T0330573

Everyday Agri-Environmental Governance

Revitalising the way the social sciences question agri-environmental governance, this book introduces "the everyday governance approach" as a means to improving the sustainability of agriculture and food systems.

The "everyday" refers to localised practices, specific networks, and practical norms that emerge in a process of interaction, translation, and reinterpretation. The authors build this approach on assemblage thinking and theory, which focuses on the collective production of the social through complex sets of connections. For this reason, assemblage thinking becomes a particularly productive guide in exploring how everyday governance is co-produced in the interaction between numerous social processes involving a diversity of actors and instruments. The authors navigate between original and contrasting case studies from Switzerland, Indonesia, and the European Union in order to reorient attention to the transformative nature of governance, which they locate along four different dimensions of the everyday: (1) the interdependence of instruments within a wider governance assemblage; (2) the uncertainty and unpredictability of effects in agri-environmental governance; (3) the distributed nature of agency and its implication for power relations; (4) the importance of capacities in the transformation of agri-food systems. This book calls for a redesigning of agri-environmental governance that should move away from the setting of fix and precise objectives and solutions, and rather aim for a consolidation of sound foundations on which desirable futures can emerge.

The book will be an essential read for students and scholars interested in sustainable agriculture and food systems, governance modes and approaches, and sustainability more broadly.

Jérémie Forney is a Full Professor at the Anthropology Institute of the University of Neuchâtel, Switzerland. He is the co-author of *Agri-environmental Governance as an Assemblage* (Routledge, 2018).

Dana Bentia is an Associate Researcher at the Anthropology Institute of the University of Neuchâtel, Switzerland.

Angga Dwiartama is an Associate Professor in Biomanagement in the School of Life Sciences and Technology at the Institut Teknologi Bandung, Indonesia.

Routledge Focus on Environment and Sustainability

For more information about this series, please visit: www.routledge.com/Routledge-Focus-on-Environment-and-Sustainability/book-series/RFES

Everyday Agri-Environmental Governance

The Emergence of Sustainability through Assemblage Thinking

Jérémie Forney, **Dana Bentia**, **and Angga Dwiartama**

Routledge
Taylor & Francis Group

LONDON AND NEW YORK

from Routledge

First published 2025
by Routledge
4 Park Square, Milton Park, Abingdon, Oxon OX14 4RN

and by Routledge
605 Third Avenue, New York, NY 10158

Routledge is an imprint of the Taylor & Francis Group, an informa business

Funded by Swiss National Science Foundation

British Library Cataloguing-in-Publication Data
A catalogue record for this book is available from the British Library

ISBN: 978-1-032-22132-8 (hbk)
ISBN: 978-1-032-84324-7 (pbk)
ISBN: 978-1-003-27126-0 (ebk)

DOI: 10.4324/9781003271260

Typeset in Times New Roman
by Newgen Publishing UK

Contents

Preface and acknowledgement

This book emerges from multiple encounters and relations that develop around long research engagement with agri-environmental governance (AEG). The three authors shared an equal passion for food and agriculture matters, and a similar conviction that the answers provided by our societies to achieve sustainable food futures are often pushing in the wrong directions. AEG has become a tentacular, polymorphous, penetrating, and sometimes alienating entity of control and surveillance, too often losing sight of its fundamental objectives to concentrate on control and measurements *per se*. With these preoccupations in mind, Jérémie Forney launched, at the University of Neuchâtel in 2015, the project "New directions in agri-environmental governance: re-assembling food, knowledge and autonomy", which was funded generously by the Swiss National Sciences Foundation. The authors want to acknowledge and say thank you for this important support. Dana Bentia joined the project in 2016 and contributed to its development, together with two PhD students, Ismaël Tall and Thomas Vetter. The excellent spirit animating the research team has been inspirational, as well as each one's deep engagement with the everyday of a concrete example of AEG. Many great scholars contributed to the thoughts and discussions developed in Neuchâtel. Angga Dwiartama was one of them and he also joined the team for an extension of the research project engaging with AEG and digitalisation. But many more have nurtured our work with their critical comments and insightful suggestions. We want to thank, in particular, Michael Carolan, Hugh Campbell, and Terry Marsden for their long-lasting and stimulating partnership developed in the context of the project. Thanks also to Nadine Arnold, Ronan Le Velly, Damian Maye, Katja Neves, Christoph Oberlack, Katrin Prager, Rikke Stotten, Gisela Welz, Michael Winter, and Steven Wolf for their participation in the workshops and colloquium associated with the project. Finally, Jérémie Forney wishes to also thank the team of the Anthropology Institute at the University of Neuchâtel, particularly Ellen Hertz and Marion Fresia. Their friendly support has been crucial for this book to have the possibility to emerge, and their contributions have been more influential in the process than they might think.

1 Everyday agri-environmental governance and the assemblage perspective

Introduction: the messy processes of agri-environmental governance

From its early stages, questions about the impacts of modern agriculture on political stability, national defence, or natural-resource management and conservation have been constantly raised. In response, governments, private actors, and civil society have followed up with answers to address the faults or fragilities of what has been seen as a strategic and problematic sector. Modern agriculture has since become a field of intense interventions by which several actors seek to steer its evolution towards what they see as a better and more desirable future. The emergence of the "environment" as a political object in the second part of the twentieth century (as signified by Carson's Silent Spring, 1963), together with the establishment of "sustainable development" as a leading concept (Brundtland, 1989), both for public policy and private business strategy, have partly reshaped the way these interventions were imagined and designed. Governance interventions have grown in number and diversified in nature to address issues relating to food, agriculture, and the environmental dimension of sustainability, in a context of deregulation and re-regulation often associated to neoliberal inspirations (e.g. Bain et al., 2005; Lockie & Higgins, 2007; Potter & Tilzey, 2007).

Since the 1980s, the governance of agriculture and food systems has gone through an "ecologisation" turn (Lamine, 2011) in many countries and at the global level too, with a progressive integration of the framing of sustainability into national policies, international regulations, and private-based instruments such as certification schemes and standards (see Hatanaka et al., 2005). This turn followed diverse paces and degrees of integration, depending on country-specific political and

DOI: 10.4324/9781003271260-1

economic contexts, while other agendas remained prominent and even antagonistic to environmental objectives. Agri-environmental governance (AEG), understood as a "broad framing that encompasses the multiple actions, which aim to implement change in the food system and address environmental issues related to agricultural production" (Forney et al., 2018: 2), has become a major field of intervention for a growing number of actors, at a large variety of scales, and through numerous modes of action.

However, despite the multiplication of actions, regulations, and initiatives, environmental issues related to food production, processing, and consumption have not disappeared. On the contrary, our knowledge of the problems has continuously deepened, pointing to, for instance, the fundamental role of agriculture in the dramatic decline of biodiversity, notably through the destruction of habitats (CBD, 2014), and in climate change, through the emission of greenhouse gases (IPCC, 2019). At the same time, food and agriculture are certainly among the sectors most exposed to the consequences of these environmental changes, which manifest by menacing soil fertility, access to water and other natural resources, and other ecosystem services that are essential to their good functioning. While complex and globalised food systems become structurally exposed to crises at the global and local scales (Lang, 2010), the diagnosis of this failure (Rosin et al., 2011) becomes obviously related to a failure of environmental governance, not limited to food systems (Arnouts & Arts, 2009). Such a statement stresses the utmost importance of rethinking how governance is done in practice and thought of in theory, while also supporting new ways of understanding change and building solutions. This is the difficult task that we engage with in this book.

One of our starting points builds on the statement that, while we understand governance as the various ways development objectives are pursued, power is exercised, and changes are planned through an act of governing, we overlook the messy processes underlying how governance is made and immersed into the everyday lives of people who are influenced by it. From meeting rooms and computer software to paddocks and farms, governance in agriculture, food, and the environment involves many elements that interfere and collaborate in producing what becomes governance, when considered beyond simple narratives of change and instead as a complex set of relations.

To capture the complexity of AEG, we acknowledge the authoritative literature on governance brought by Michel Foucault (1979) through the idea of governmentality. Governmentality is understood as the art of governance, or ways in which one (government, individuals, corporation) exerts control over others through apparatuses, tactics, and procedures. Tania Li's book *The Will to Improve* (2007b) expands the notion of governmentality into the context of development, environmental governance, and forest conservation in her case of Indonesia. In her book, Li demonstrates the messy process of governance that goes a long way in history through the involvement of multiple actors, including the state, academics, experts, NGOs, and international donor agencies.

In governmentality, Foucault argues for distinctive modes of governance across history, from sovereign, disciplinary, to the current neoliberal form of governmentality, which is dictated by market mechanisms, liberal democracies, and the de-centring of power. In reference to this, Rose (1996) also sees neoliberal governmentality as a form of advanced liberal way of governance, whereby the state transforms its governing strategies from welfare approach into choices of individual citizens, therefore narrowing down the role of the state and the collective role of society. This view is later criticised by Stenson and Watt (1999), who posit the idea of hybrid governance. In their view, even within the neoliberal approach to governance, the role of the "social" is not necessarily diminished, but instead reformulated through an assemblage of rationalities. Higgins and Lockie (2002) further elaborate on this through their case of natural resource management and AEG in Australia, wherein the distinction between neoliberal and other modes of governance is no longer visible. Here, the authors offer a more nuanced form of environmental governance calling for an analytical lens that would be better equipped to speak of the blurry and messy nature of governance, beyond fixed and pre-existing categorisations.

At the basis of a new way of engaging with governance, we propose the concept of everyday governance as an answer to: the limitations of classical approaches to governance; an implicit understanding of social change as linear which fails to answer the unpredictable nature of change; an artificial and ideological split between public policies and private governance; the unresolved tensions between explanations drawing on structural power relations and others emphasising the role of subjectivity and agency. We set the scene of AEG as a major issue for the future of more-than-human societies—which means new ways of living and thinking human societies with non-humans.

Governance practices are often based on assumptions and more or less idealised visions of how things should be and how to get there. Many approaches to and credos about how to make things change can be found: new technologies, consumers' responsibility, farmers' education, regulation or deregulation, etc. We call for better articulation between narratives opposed to this projective understanding of governance. We assert that governance results from the encounter of diverse instruments and localised sets of daily and concrete interactions. The notion of everyday governance allows us to analyse the outcomes of governance practices beyond ideas of success and failure, and therefore leaves room to explore the multiplicity and complexity of processes by looking at governance in its daily social production. In addition, an everyday-governance perspective adopts the points of view of the actors. This results in a discussion and problematisation of the categories usually used in analyses of AEG in diverse geographical and political contexts.

Supporting such an approach requires us to find a theoretical framework to engage with messiness and complexity across the usual boundaries and categories. We found in assemblage thinking a fertile ground on which we can sow and cultivate concepts that would capture what is at stake in governance from an everyday perspective. The seminal work of Deleuze and Guattari (1988) has inspired many developments and translations in more recent literature (e.g. Bennett, 2010; Buchanan, 2021; Callon, 2017; DeLanda, 2016). Assemblage thinking and assemblage theory have already penetrated diverse fields of research related to AEG, such as the anthropology of globalisation (e.g. Ong & Collier, 2005), critical development studies (e.g. Li, 2007a), or agri-food studies (e.g. Forney et al., 2018; Rosin et al., 2017; Loconto, 2015). In this book, we propose to build on this existing literature, along with diverse empirical examples, to carve paths that could lead us out of some of the dead ends which AEG seems to be locked in.

Exploring the everyday dimension of AEG

How should we engage with the everyday dimension of AEG? To begin with, let us imagine three hypothetical situations, or *stories*, which are inspired by our empirical work on AEG, in which everyday governance is enacted through practical encounters, conflicts, negotiations, dilemmas, agreements, and reflections.

Story 1: Nicolas,[1] navigating the Swiss AEG assemblage

Nicolas is a farmer in the lowlands of Switzerland. On his farm, he raises a few beef cattle. Besides the pastures, grassland, and a few hectares of corn used to feed the cows, he cultivates crops of wheat, spelt, and rapeseed certified under the IP-Suisse label. Today, Nicolas has sown wheat on a field that he sprayed with a herbicide a few days ago. This "cleaning" of the weeds is the only chemical intervention allowed by the label and the agri-environmental scheme for an "extensive" wheat production he subscribed to and for which he will get state money. The combination of the premium price paid for the label and the subsidies received, interestingly, compensates for the loss in productivity. And he saves the cost of the additional chemicals and the petrol for the tractor he would have incurred for further treatments. At the side of the field, a hedgerow and a few piles of stones supposedly offer a beneficial environment for biodiversity. They are part of the IP-Suisse biodiversity programme. The hedgerow is also registered in the regional "ecological network", which unites biodiversity infrastructures installed on all the neighbouring farms: another programme supported by the agricultural policy. Driving home, Nicolas passes by the sloping plot of land on which he planted 50 trees last year under a scheme supporting agroforestry practices. Since he left dairy production eight years ago, when he took over the family farm, the pasture has not been in much need. Given the crash of milk prices that followed the dismantling of the state-based quota system, quitting the dairy industry was certainly a good move. All this makes him think of Olivier, his friend who remained a passionate dairy farmer, but has found himself stuck on his too-small farm with no access to additional land and little flexibility to participate in similar programmes. Olivier needs all of his land to feed his cows, but this prevents him from compensating for the low milk prices with the money from additional environmental schemes. Nicolas thinks that he himself has found a nice balance between the push for more environmentally friendly agricultural practices and his fundamental motivation to produce food for the people.

Story 2: Novelina and Harbin, telling agents in the soybean assemblage

A group of twenty people are visiting a soybean field at an agronomic research institute in Western Switzerland. Novelina and Harbin are the two seed varieties being tested this year. They have grown well despite rather dry conditions during spring, and many innovative adjustments in their cultivation proved beneficial for their development. These seeds have been adapted for the last fifteen years to be able to ripe naturally without desiccation. The basis of these breakthroughs is research that received national support in the 80s, at a time when "it was quite mad to begin because very few people were aware of this delicate and versatile plant". There is thus reason to celebrate that currently, many farmers, seed breeders, and various industries and businesses from across Europe seek to integrate these and other varieties of soybeans in their plans and actions. Yet change is difficult, as there are many barriers along the way, markets are competitive, costs are high, trust is low, there are clashing arguments over standards being either too high or not high enough, and there is this sense that Europe is struggling at the policy level. At the same time, there is evidence from many countries that national plans support legume development and its various qualities needed in terms of its use for soils, feed, oils, and food. Enthusiasm grows time and time again, when there is news of a powerful farming association deciding to use the new standard after taking five years to make this step, or when important advocates against deforestation support the work being done for sustainable soy. Indeed, the momentum for change is here, and anything can happen, a dialogue between producing and consuming countries is emerging and Brazil even starts to imagine a possible switch and transition to organic soy production. During the lunch break, a Serbian soybean farmer is checking his emails to be surprised by an invitation from the association he had recently become a member of to join a study trip to China, to learn about the roots of soybeans. He immediately decides to register and is so happy to have a special opportunity to visit the unique wild soybean seed varieties bank he always dreamt of seeing.

Story 3: Fitri and the messy assemblage of public governance

Fitri[2] is a public civil servant working for a regional environmental agency in Indonesia. She oversees the applications for development projects and the extent to which environmental compliance has been fulfilled. In a day, she receives hundreds of applications of that sort. Not only does she have to assess how companies plan their environmental management, Fitri also has to coordinate with other government agencies on how implementing those projects would compromise missed land potentials, be they related to agriculture, forestry, dwellings, road infrastructure, tourism, or nature preservation. In one instance, she argues with her colleague from the Agricultural Agency about the best possible way to utilise fallow land. Food security is indeed essential—and agriculture, therefore, should be a solution, but so should the protection of forests, watersheds, and wildlife in the surrounding area. The current spatial plan has not seriously taken the environment into consideration, and Fitri wishes that there were a grand design for environmental planning that would be on top of every development plan in the region. While in Europe, for instance, a multifunctional agriculture (one that integrates biodiversity and nature preservation) can become a beneficial scheme, Indonesia needs a stricter, top-down solution to Fitri's dilemma: one purpose for one patch of land. The idea seems straightforward, but Fitri overlooks the complexity behind a simple environmental grand design—piling up data, spatial plans, development goals, and project proposals one on top of the other, as well as connecting to a massive network of stakeholders. It would have been easier to let spatial planning do its work and focus on individual projects, assessing their environmental impacts and ways to mitigate these impacts. Yet, she knows that less economically appealing land-use projects such as agriculture and food production or nature reserves would have gone unnoticed amidst larger development projects such as mining, manufacturing, or real estate. So, a grand design for an environmental management plan makes sense. What Fitri and many like her in the environmental or planning offices are facing is a novel approach to agri-environmental governance that may or may not work, but is (designed to be) profound and transformative nonetheless.

Everyday governance as framing

These snapshots from the daily lives of these two fictional human actors, Nicolas and Fitri, and the destiny of the non-human soya bean *Novelina* and *Harbin*, are illustrative of the many complex relations in which individuals (both humans and non-humans) find themselves in the context of the governance of environmental issues within agriculture and food production. An everyday perspective on governance begins with this messiness of individual situations and the many relations that characterise them. Starting from a field of wheat, a soya bean, or lines on a map, uncountable ramifications connect the many actors and elements involved in the making of public policies, certification schemes, environmental plans, and other endeavours aimed at steering agriculture and food systems towards more sustainable and desirable futures. These intense sets of relations can be usefully understood as AEG assemblages, and this is one of the main points we will demonstrate in this book.

Diverse regulations, schemes, and actions come together and merge in the everyday. From these encounters, localised practices, specific networks, and practical norms emerge in the process of inter-action, translation, and reinterpretation that has been called "everyday governance" by anthropologists such as Agrawal and Gibson (1999) and Blundo (Blundo, 2002; Blundo & Le Meur, 2009). Consequently, an everyday perspective examines how AEG is produced through repeated interaction between diverse human actors and other elements constituting an AEG assemblage. From an everyday perspective, governance is a whole in which individuals are entangled and diverse categories are fused together. There is no clear separation between the everyday experience of public policy schemes and private standards; the connections that develop around soya traverse national and sectoral boundaries; the attempt to reorganise planning through data involves not only multi-sectoral coordination but also inter-regional governance. Here the everyday perspective rejoins "an emergent theorisation of assemblage [in the AEG literature]—never fully defined and bounded, but always seeking to destabilise existing categories and constraints on the multiplicity of actors, power and process" (Forney et al., 2018: 10).

The original inspiration for this book can be found in the authors' previous research on AEG practices that led to the identification of several weaknesses and limitations in the way our current societies develop answers to agri-environmental issues and challenges. Drawing on long-term fieldwork and research in Switzerland, we could, for instance, identify three issues in the current AEG panoply developed in this country, but also in a more global context: "an enduring disconnection between the main steps in the food production; the lack of new knowledge creation among the actors involved in the reality of agri-environmental practices; and the lack of autonomy in a very controlled food system" (Forney, 2016: 2).

By moving away from "classical approaches" to governance, this book argues that thinking through an everyday- and assemblage-theory-informed approach can help us, in a practical sense, solve issues around bureaucratisation, silo thinking, linear thinking, rigid goal-oriented approach, and other recurring problems in governance (Ferguson, 1994). In Chapter 3 of this book, for instance, we demonstrate how unpredictability and uncertainty should be seen as an integral part of governance, which can be well comprehended and anticipated if we shy away from a linear way of thinking about cause and effect. Consequently, this leads us to rethink the very concept of change and transformation, as elaborated further in Chapter 5. An everyday perspective takes us beyond the bureaucratic and command-control approach to governance, by understanding that agency and power lie not within the (powerful) actors but distributed across human and non-human actors, as well as through their complex relations. In practice, this viewpoint enables us to comprehend the diverse ways governance is directed: top down, bottom up, sideways, and across sectors. Chapter 4 explores this in more detail.

While the everyday perspective enables us to start our investigation into AEG from a different point of departure, we also need a different way of thinking about relations that build into governance. As mentioned earlier, our alternative comprehension of uncertainties, agency, power, and change pivots around assemblage thinking, which opens new possibilities for thinking differently of problems and responses.

Reframing everyday governance as an assemblage

Assemblage has become a very popular word in academic writing for some years now. However, this often comes with a superficial level of engagement with what it could mean at the level of theory and how this theory can nurture practices and action in the "real world".

Most of the time, "assemblage" or "assembling" is used to refer to any "collection of things", and Buchanan (2021: 3) pertinently questions the very point of using a concept for such a vague idea. Hertz (2016) also questioned this passion for fancy concepts in the literature, often hiding, indeed, quite simple ideas. However, both authors, in their ways, defend a more productive and useful activation of concepts. Buchanan sets out to defend the value of a theory of assemblage by engaging deeply with the work of Deleuze and Guattari. Hertz gives examples where concepts and theorisation are actually producing analyses that would be difficult to develop without them.

In this book, we are closer to Hertz's take on the use of the concepts. Following a "pragmatic" conception of social theory as "a collection of generalizing tricks" (Becker, 1998: 12), we suggest moving the focus from a "theory of assemblage"—even if we will draw on authors such as Buchanan, who actually engaged in fundamental theorisations—to analytical explorations around the uses and efficacy of assemblage as a conceptual framing. From this perspective, theoretical constructs and concepts are not a goal or achievement in themselves, but only "something we need in order to get our work done" (Becker, 1998: 12). Concepts allow us to engage better with the messiness and complexity of the social, and "to come to more accurate, and not simply more interesting, accounts of the world we live in" (Hertz, 2016: 156). To build such a "pragmatic" assemblage approach is somehow counterintuitive, given the highly abstract and theoretical nature of the seminal work by Deleuze and Guattari (1988) on assemblage. Fortunately, many authors have contributed to the process and translated their seminal thoughts into more operational and structured propositions. This stance on theory is not that far away from what Deleuze himself says in dialogue with Foucault, where he calls theory a box of tools, emphasising its need to be useful and functional (cf. Buchanan, 2021: 7).

Let us consider that an assemblage describes an entity as a complex set of lines and relations between heterogeneous elements, which are all interconnected. This assemblage has no real centre. Its elements are not hierarchically organised and often belong simultaneously to other assemblages. This assemblage is, therefore, connected to others through these multiple belongings. It crosses over scales and distances, as do the connections it is made of. It has no a priori geographical or institutional boundaries. In some ways, this assemblage has no definite beginning or end. As Anna Tsing (2015: 83) puts it, an assemblage is "an open-ended entanglement of ways of being". At the same time, assemblage as a concept has to refer to irreducible wholes in order to replace more efficiently essentialising totalities, such as the state or the market (DeLanda, 2016: 11–13). The irreducibility and the open-ended nature that characterise assemblages are easier to combine than we might think at first. Indeed, there is no need to know precisely all the pieces of a whole to start exploring its properties. In fact, an assemblage approach is more interested in tracking lines of relations than in building boundaries or adding up all existing elements one by one.

Any assemblage consists of elements (humans and non-humans) that are physically attached and held together. This is what Deleuze and Guattari refer to as a machinic assemblage. However, this machinic assemblage also intertwines with an expression of meanings and desires through the becoming of the assemblage, referred to as an assemblage of enunciation. To this, an assemblage approach repositions the question of what something or someone is as produced by its/her/his inclusion within a set of interactions and relations. In this sense, elements or individuals are expressions of multiplicities—they are made of their multiple belongings. Equally, who or what someone/something "is" can be understood when we consider the multiplicities in which he/she/it participates. In Deleuze and Guattari's words:

> There are no individual statements, there never are. Every statement is the product of a machinic assemblage, in other words, of collective agents of enunciation (take "collective agents" to mean not peoples or societies but multiplicities). The proper name (*nom propre*) does not designate an individual: it is on the contrary when the individual opens up to the multiplicities pervading him or her, at the outcome of the most severe operation of depersonalization, that he or she acquires his or her true proper name.
>
> (1988: 37)

This echoes the idea of *emergence*, which is central to what Urry calls the complexity turn to which assemblage approaches, and other Deleuzian theorisations, are related (Urry, 2005). The properties of an assemblage are produced by the interactions between its parts and therefore are always more than the addition of the properties of its parts (DeLanda, 2016: 9). Connections and relations are unstable things. Therefore, assemblages need continuous effort to be maintained, stabilised, or "territorialised" (in the metaphorical sense used by Deleuze and Guattari, with no relation to geographical territories). *Territorialisation* (which consists of a concurrent process of de- and reterritorialisation) refers to a cognitive act of coordination, involving continuous weakening and reinforcing processes within an entity. In the book *Anti-Oedipus* (1983), Deleuze and Guattari refer to a territory as a conceptual environment (not necessarily a physical space) that facilitates stable social relations, but whose boundaries invariably change as an assemblage takes shape. An assemblage is therefore ephemeral and only being stable through "a continuous process to create a quasi-stable state" (Dwiartama & Piatti, 2016: 157).

For the same reason, assemblages are always prone to change and subject to transforming forces. Those forces are brought in by its elements that push and pull the whole assemblage along *lines of flight* (and the concurrent *lines of articulation*), creating "movements of deterritorialisation" (and reterritorialisation) (Deleuze & Guatarri, 1988), or by previously external elements that join the assemblage. In other words, an assemblage approach pays attention not only to how things are organised and connected but also, and maybe above all, to the processes of change and stabilisation at work. As Dittmer (2014: 388) puts it, this dynamism "means that a range of contingent futures is always possible". An assemblage is not only what is in the present time. It is also what it tends towards, what it might become. It is made of the whole set of forces trying to reshape it. In this sense, assemblages participate in an ontology of multiplicities and future possibilities.

Everyday governance: from instruments to assemblages

In order to operationalise the theoretical framing offered by assemblage thinking, there is a need for more empirical concepts. We suggest drawing on the political sociology of governance, inspired notably by a "tools approach" to public policies (Salamon & Lund, 1989), and looking at AEG assemblages through the description and analysis of its instrumentation (Lascoumes & Le Galès, 2007), expanding the use of the concept also to other types of governance practices, not only public policies. This means using a broad definition of governance "instruments" as organised sets of rules, good practices, metrologies, and procedures, articulated and developed in order to exercise social control over a targeted population and to influence practices.

Approaching AEG assemblages through instruments means identifying practices that form an identified instrument, while focusing on how it interacts with and connects to other governance instruments in a wider governance assemblage. Instruments are fractions of a governance assemblage, they can be used as a necessary framing and focus to develop an analysis. They offer a starting point from which the multiple relations making the assemblage can be traced, and its complexity can be reconstructed. Nevertheless, these fragments are always understood as elements of a more abstract whole, through the lens of their relations with other instruments and actors.

While an assemblage follows no real boundaries and crosses over any pre-accepted categories of governance, instruments are attached to institutions and tend to reproduce existing social categories, at least on the face of it. For example, a specific direct payment scheme is framed as a public-policy instrument, as part of a state-based agricultural policy. However, looking at it from an assemblage perspective will probably reveal how it interacts with other governance tools, some offering obvious connections (other aspects of the same agricultural policies) and others being more distant (e.g. environmental standards set by retailers), as well as integrating the role of multiple agents who help to translate an instrument into concrete practices.

The analysis of the instrument explores how its design and materiality shape the interplay between the multiple agents, how those agents use it and reinterpret it in their daily practice, and how different socio-economic and political logics develop through these multiple interactions. An instrument develops within a given network of actors, creating new ties and re-establishing older ones, but its effects might spill over these limits. An instrument is generally developed for a specific task, with a specific goal, but as Lascoumes and Le Galès (2007: 1) point out, "[instruments] produce specific effects, independently of the objective pursued (the aims ascribed to them)". The final objective cannot be to fully understand an AEG assemblage in its totality. Indeed, as we suggested, there are no real ways to define fixed boundaries, to delineate clearly an assemblage, as it is always moving and changing, and because the relations it is made up of are never really ending. Rather, looking at AEG assemblages through AEG instruments aims to reposition specific practices in their wider assemblage context. It offers a way to look at elements, while acknowledging that they cannot be understood outside the relations they are made of.

Looking at what is happening within and beyond an instrument and its application from an assemblage perspective means acknowledging a double movement: first, the diverse effects resulting from the application of an instrument are products of a wider assemblage and cannot be understood from the instrument perspective only. Second, instruments and their evolution affect the wider assemblage in which they participate in relation—tensions, synergies, influences, etc.—with other elements of this assemblage. These theoretical considerations are of great importance at a more practical level of governance: they imply that no isolated instrument will offer a solution to problems by itself. Innovations in the design of governance tools and instruments will certainly impact the wider governance assemblage, but will also be shaped and transformed by its insertion within a complex set of governance practices. Therefore, innovation in governance should include from the beginning this interactive, and context-specific, dimension. Similarly, the expectations for changes and transformations resulting from the governance action should be distributed across a changing and evolving assemblage and not only focus on the one new practice that may be introduced.

Consequently, analysing and assessing the effects and outcomes of a specific instrument as part of a wider ever-changing assemblage implies looking beyond direct and clear impacts and opening the perspective to more subtle, indirect, and sinuous lines of effects, for example in forms of small changes. A good way to do so is to adopt an empirical approach to governance from the perspective of the agents' everyday lives within the governance assemblage. Human and non-human actors experience the assemblage as a whole. Beyond individual instruments and their design and materiality, localised practices, specific networks, and practical norms emerge in a process of interaction, translation, and reinterpretation that anthropologists have called "everyday governance" (Agrawal & Gibson, 1999; Blundo, 2002; Blundo & Le Meur, 2009). Such an approach is based on ethnographic methods used to understand holistically what governance practices produce in real life. The objective has generally been to understand how transversal logics of governance develop in specific contexts and to pay more attention to how people play with rules, interpret and divert them—in other words, how they engage with governance. In association with an assemblage perspective, the everyday governance becomes a way to anchor specific instruments within a wider governance assemblage. This grounded approach to the governance analysis refers to a framing that considers governance more as actions rather than ideas. Looking at AEG practices through an assemblage lens means highlighting this openness and the embeddedness in wider assemblages; it means focusing not so much on the specificities of the elements but rather on the multiple connections that make them exist in the whole.

How we use case studies in this book

With this perspective in mind, it is therefore necessary for us to build our argument through empirical case studies based on an ethnography of everyday lives. Just as the three *ethnofictions* given previously set the scene for an everyday engagement with different forms of AEG, we aim to mobilise three specific cases that illustrate how assemblage thinking may offer a different lens to how we normally perceive, and practice, governance. The three cases—an agri-environmental certification scheme in Switzerland (IP-Suisse), a large strategic programme towards soybean production in the Danube river basin (Donau Soja), and the introduction of a new environmental management plan in Indonesia (RPPLH)—offer a broad range of geographies, scales, focal points, and typologies. For one thing, this diversity reflects one of the AEG practices currently implemented globally. Let us, however, make it clear that our cases by no means offer a generic pattern of governance, nor represent the globally diverse governance practices. They are also far from being seen as good practices, although some may prove to be more successful than others.

The rationale behind the choice of our case studies stems from our long-term research work and ethnographic engagement with the farmers, government agencies, business sectors, technocrats, and grassroots movements that shape the whole stories of this everyday governance (Forney, 2016; Forney et al., 2018, 2023; Bentia & Forney, 2018; Bentia, 2021a, 2021b; Dwiartama, 2018; Forney & Dwiartama, 2023). We reflect not only on their experiences and viewpoints but also on how they help us navigate between theory and empirics. In a way, these cases are partly illustrative of, but also the source of inspiration for, how we build our deeper understandings of assemblage thinking. Although previous studies use assemblage thinking to highlight some of the key aspects of our cases (path dependency, human–nonhuman relations, Deleuzian society of control), it is in this book that we seek to build a rather comprehensive description of the governance assemblages and, by doing so, experiment with novel ways of working with assemblage theory.

What is also important to note here is that, as a methodological tool, assemblage thinking relies on "description" as a particular kind of "mapping", as a cartographic exercise that directs our analysis to the elements and relations performed at a certain moment in time and in a particular context (Anderson et al., 2012). In using assemblage as a *descriptor*, our cases demonstrate that, although we can always understand any entity through its relationality (and therefore as an assemblage), not all "relational understanding" can be claimed to represent assemblage thinking. For instance, we avoid seeing relations as necessarily stable, or that the parts constitute a whole—a system, if you will (as with systems theory). When we talk about IP-Suisse, Donau Soja, or RPPLH, we do not see them as examples of a homogenous or singular body of organisation that reinforces its boundaries, but instead as "the bringing together of heterogeneous entities into some form of temporary relation" (Anderson et al., 2012: 177). Insofar as we do not look at our cases as best practices, we are fortunate to capture a significant number of characteristics (messiness, unpredictability, non-linearity, ephemerality of relations) that make a learning case for assemblage thinking, and can nurture, we believe, new ways of doing governance. This helps us to demonstrate how these characteristics participate in changing elements, relations, and processes, and also how they are essential to, and define, the "mechanics" of the assemblage.

This leads us to understand assemblage as *ethos* (Anderson et al., 2012; Adey, 2012). Assemblage thinking helps us to engage with governance in a specific way, one that brings practical implications too. Just like theories of care brought a turn towards the politics of care and non-representation in feminist social theories (Puig de La Bellacasa, 2015), there is a moral imperative about how AEG ought to be practised that brings an emancipatory turn to agency (Stirling, 2015). Assemblage thinking gives a voice to those everyday actors that are not so much "important" decision-makers, but who do stretch and shape the boundaries of the governance assemblage nonetheless (see Chapter 4). It also enables us to move beyond a path-dependent logic and embrace the unpredictability of outcomes as the norm, rather than the exception, in the current state of environmental governance. In Chapter 6, we therefore bring that "ethos of engagement that attends to the messiness and complexity of phenomena" (Adey, 2012: 198) by shifting, among others, from an objective to relational measurement, from centralised to distributed responsibilities, and from prediction to unpredictability and ensuing reorientation to other governance targets.

Structure of the book

This book, therefore, synthesises our way of rethinking governance and transformation in the environment, agriculture, and food systems, through the lens of assemblage. While through our empirical cases we engage more deeply with the theory (thus using assemblage as a concept and descriptor), our aim is to offer ways to mobilise our cases as a useful insight into how we can co-construct the future of governance practices. In each of the empirical chapters (chapters 2–5), we tell the stories of IP-Suisse, Donau Soja, and RPPLH intertwiningly, while highlighting the convergence that leads to a certain aspect of assemblage thinking, but simultaneously the divergence that indicates how versatile and fluid an assemblage can be.

In Chapter 2, we illustrate what our cases look like when we see them as assemblages. The chapter moves from a more structural depiction of the entities at the start of the chapter to a more fluid, boundary-less set of relations among heterogeneous elements at the end. By unravelling these messy entanglements, we make our case that governance is not as strict and straightforward as it is too often perceived. While we build our case studies, we also reintroduce some of the language of assemblage thinking, including lines of flight, lines of articulation, territorialisation, and multiplicity.

Chapter 3 elaborates on the ontological consequences of employing assemblage thinking for our cases. Instead of focusing on the success and failure of a certain governance programme, we look at how the unpredictability of effects is an integral part of an assemblage. We use notions like lines of flight, overflows, and un-intentionality to show that what emerges from governance practices goes far beyond their explicit goals, and that the question is not so much one of achievement. The cases illustrate how the unintended effects of an assemblage may help in bringing a new and emergent set of relations. When we look through the lens of assemblage, we may learn to anticipate unpredictable effects and be more adaptive to the ephemerality of a governance assemblage.

What is also critical in the use of assemblage thinking is how it offers a different lens for understanding agency and power. Chapter 4 discusses this in more detail, shifting away from a structural (and even Foucauldian) sense of agency to the interplay between individual, collective, and distributive agency. What connects this notion of power/ agency is desire, emanating not only from human actors but also from non-human elements and even the assemblage itself. Desire drives elements to either cofunction or break away (or both). In our cases, not only does agency shape an assemblage, but the assemblage itself shapes how individual agency is manifested, such as through the power of a document, a label, meetings, or data.

Both the unpredictability of effects and the shaping of desires lead us to question what change is from an assemblage perspective. In Chapter 5, we see change as a norm—where stability is instead the exception. However, we do not see change (and transformation) through a unilinear path. We understand it in its diverse trajectories within a space of possibility, which emerges from the encounter of the properties, capacities, and desires characterising an assemblage. This helps us clarify what unpredictability means: while it is impossible to fully predict change, some level of anticipation is still possible as an assemblage does not follow randomly in any trajectory. Here, we raise the notion of attractor. An attractor guides change and the evolution of the assemblage in interplay with desires. Multiple attractors generally influence the course of change, forming a basin of attraction. Our cases thus show that by identifying these attractors, we may be able to partly anticipate the transformation pathway an AEG assemblage will follow in the future.

Our last chapter (Chapter 6) serves as a pragmatic implication for using assemblage thinking and everyday governance. How can we mobilise all of this understanding of assemblage in the construction of future governance practices? Although we refrain from prescribing a guideline, we identify four principles as points of departure for building a new form of governance. Here, we expand from the reflexive governance paradigm, as a very important basis, to propose a *governance of emergence*. This form of governance shifts towards redistributing responsibilities, embracing relational monitoring methods, experimenting with spaces of possibilities, and moving away from prediction to targeting attractors.

Our book seems to leave little doubt that the second decade of the twenty-first century is marked by a wider awareness of the weighty dark shadow of past human actions. This realisation has created an impulse for action manifested in terms of eager planning for brighter near futures: constellations for biodiversity (as shown in the case of IP-Suisse), for an alternate pathways in global agriculture (as in the case of Donau Soja), and for a new understanding of data and coordination (as in RPPLH). The present, though, is characterised by far less clarity of purpose and unequivocal action trajectories, where both the visible and invisible dynamics ensue. Assemblage thinking may help us navigate our everyday practices of governance through this uncertain and unpredictable future.

Notes

1 Nicolas and Oliver are fictional characters built on the basis of Swiss farmers' real accounts and stories about their own experiences and lives.
2 Likewise, Fitri is the personification of many government officials that are at the forefront of a transformation in the realm of environmental policies in Indonesia.

References

Adey, P. (2012). How to engage? Assemblage as ethos/ethos as assemblage. *Dialogues in Human Geography* 2(2): 198–201.

Agrawal, A., & Gibson, C. C. (1999). Enchantment and disenchantment: the role of community in natural resource conservation. *World Development* 27(4): 629–649.

Anderson, B., Kearnes, M., McFarlane, C., & Swanton, D. (2012). On assemblages and geography. *Dialogues in Human Geography* 2(2): 171–189.

Arnouts, R., & Arts, B. (2009). Environmental governance failure: the "dark side" of an essentially optimistic concept. In B. Arts, A. Lagendijk, & H. van Houtum (Eds.). *The Desoriented State: Shifts in Governmentality, Territoriality and Governance*. Berlin: Springer.

Bain, C., Deaton, B., & Busch, L. (2005). Reshaping the agri-food system: the role of standards, standard-makers and third-party certifiers. In V. Higgins & G. Lawrence (Eds.). *Agricultural Governance: Globalization and the New Politics of Regulation* (pp. 71–83). Abingdon: Routledge.

Becker, H. S. (1998). *Tricks of the Trade: How to Think about Your Research While You're Doing it*. Chicago: University of Chicago Press.

Bennett, J. (2010). *Vibrant Matter: A Political Ecology of Things*. Durham and London: Duke University Press.

Bentia, D. (2021a). Towards reconfiguration in European agriculture: analyzing dynamics of change through the lens of the Donau Soja organization. *Sociologia Ruralis* 61(4): 663–680.

Bentia, D. (2021b). Accountability beyond measurement: the role of meetings in shaping governance instruments and governance outcomes in food systems through the lens of the Danube Soy organization. *Journal of Rural Studies* 88: 50–59.

Bentia, D., & Forney, J. (2018). Beyond soyisation: Donau Soja as assemblage. In J. Forney, C. Rosin, & H. Campbell (Eds.). *Agri-Environmental Governance as an Assemblage: Multiplicity, Power, and Transformation* (pp. 177–192). London and New York: Routledge.

Blundo, G. (2002). Editorial: La gouvernance, entre technique de gouvernement et outil d'exploration empirique. *Bulletin de l'APAD [En ligne]* 23–24: 2–10.

Blundo, G., & Le Meur, P. Y. (Eds.). (2009). *The Governance of Daily Life in Africa: Ethnographic Explorations of Public and Collective Services* (Vol. 19). Leiden: Brill.

Brundtland, G. H. (1989). Global change and our common future. *Environment: Science and Policy for Sustainable Development* 31(5): 16–43.

Buchanan, I. (2021). *Assemblage Theory and Method*. London/New York: Bloomsbury.

Callon, M. (2017). *L'emprise des marchés: Comprendre leur fonctionnement pour pouvoir les changer*. Paris: La Découverte.

Carson, R. (1962). *Silent spring*. Boston: Houghton Mifflin Company.

CBD (Convention on Biological Diversity). (2014). *Global Biodiversity Outlook 4*. Montréal: Secretariat of the Convention on Biological Diversity.

DeLanda, M. (2016). *Assemblage Theory*. Edinburgh: Edinburgh University Press.

Deleuze, G., & Guattari, F. (1983). *Anti-Oedipus: Capitalism and Schizophrenia*. 1972. Trans. Robert Hurley, Mark Seem, and Helen R. Lane. Minneapolis: University of Minnesota Press.

Deleuze, G., & Guatarri, F. (1988). *A Thousand Plateaus: Capitalism and Schizophrenia*. London: Athlone.

Dittmer, J. (2014). Geopolitical assemblages and complexity. *Progress in Human Geography* 38(3): 385–401.

Dwiartama, A. (2018). From 'disciplinary societies' to 'societies of control': an historical narrative of agri-environmental governance in Indonesia. In J. Forney, C. Rosin, & H. Campbell (Eds.). *Agri-Environmental Governance as an Assemblage: Multiplicity, Power, and Transformation* (pp. 91–104). London and New York: Routledge.

Dwiartama, A., & Piatti, C. (2016). Assembling local, assembling food security. *Agriculture and Human Values* 33(1): 153–164.

Ferguson, J. (1994). *The Anti-politics Machine: Development, Depoliticization, and Bureaucratic Power in Lesotho*. Minneapolis: University of Minnesota Press.

Forney, J. (2016). Blind spots in agri-environmental governance: some reflections and suggestions from Switzerland. *Review of Agricultural, Food and Environmental Studies* 97(1): 1–13.

Forney, J., & Dwiartama, A. (2023). The project, the everyday, and reflexivity in sociotechnical agri-food assemblages: proposing a conceptual model of digitalisation. *Agriculture and Human Values* 40(2): 441–454.

Forney, J., Dwiartama, A., & Bentia, D. (2023). Everyday digitalization in food and agriculture: introduction to the symposium. *Agriculture and Human Values* 40(2): 417–421.

Forney, J., Rosin, C., & Campbell, H. (Eds.). (2018). *Agri-environmental Governance as an Assemblage: Multiplicity, Power, and Transformation.* London and New York: Routledge.

Foucault, M. (1979). "The birth of bio-politics"–Michel Foucault's lecture at the Collège de France on neo-liberal governmentality. *Economy and Society* 30(2): 190–207.

Hatanaka, M., Bain, C., & Busch, L. (2005). Third-party certification in the global agrifood system. *Food Policy* 30(3): 354–369.

Hertz, E. (2016). Pimp my fluff: a Thousand Plateaus and other theoretical extravaganzas. *Anthropological Theory* 16(2–3): 146–159.

Higgins, V., & Lockie, S. (2002). Re-discovering the social: neo-liberalism and hybrid practices of governing in rural natural resource management. *Journal of Rural Studies* 18(4): 419–428.

IPCC. (2019). Summary for policymakers. In P. R. Shukla, et al. (Eds.). *Climate Change and Land: An IPCC Special Report on Climate Change, Desertification, Land Degradation, Sustainable Land Management, Food Security, and Greenhouse Gas Fluxes in Terrestrial Ecosystems* (pp. 3–36). Intergovernmental Panel on Climate Change Secretariate.

Lamine, C. (2011). Transition pathways towards a robust ecologization of agriculture and the need for system redesign. Cases from organic farming and IPM. *Journal of Rural Studies* 27(2): 209–219.

Lascoumes, P., & Le Galès, P. (2007). Introduction: understanding public policy through its instruments—from the nature of instruments to the sociology of public policy instrumentation. *Governance* 20(1): 1–21.

Li, T. M. (2007a). Practices of assemblage and community forest management. *Economy and Society* 36(2): 263–293.

Li, T. M. (2007b). *The Will to Improve: Governmentality, Development, and the Practice of Politics.* Durham: Duke University Press.

Lockie, S., & Higgins, V. (2007). Roll-out neoliberalism and hybrid practices of regulation in Australian agri-environmental governance. *Journal of Rural Studies* 23(1): 1–11.

Loconto, A. (2015). Assembling governance: the role of standards in the Tanzanian tea industry. *Journal of Cleaner Production* 107: 64–73.

Ong, A., & Collier, S. J. (Eds.). (2005). *Global Assemblages: Technology, Politics and Ethics as Anthropological Problems*. Malden/Oxford/Victoria: Blackwell Publishing.

Potter, C., & Tilzey, M. (2007). Agricultural multifunctionality, environmental sustainability and the WTO: resistance or accommodation to the neoliberal project for agriculture? *Geoforum* 38(6): 1290–1303.

Puig De La Bellacasa, M. (2015). Making time for soil: technoscientific futurity and the pace of care. *Social Studies of Science* 45(5): 691–716.

Rose, N. (1996). Governing "advanced" liberal democracies. In A. Barry, T. Osborne, & N. Rose (Eds.). *Foucault and Political Reason: Liberalism, Neo-Liberalism and Rationalities of Government* (pp. 37–64). Chicago, IL: University of Chicago Press.

Rosin, C., Campbell, H., & Reid, J. (2017). Metrology and sustainability: using sustainability audits in New Zealand to elaborate the complex politics of measuring. *Journal of Rural Studies* 52: 90–99.

Salamon, L. M., & Lund, M. S. (1989). The tools approach: basic analytics. In L. M. Salamon (Ed.). *Beyond Privatization: The Tools of Government Action* (pp. 23–50). Washington, DC: The Urban Institute Press.

Stenson, K., & Watt, P. (1999). Governmentality and the death of the social? A discourse analysis of local government texts in Southeast England. *Urban Studies* 36(1): 189–201.

Stirling, A. (2015). Emancipating transformations: from controlling 'the transition' to culturing plural radical progress. In I. Scoones, M. Leach, & P. Newell (Eds.). *The Politics of Green Transformations* (pp. 54–67). New York/London: Routledge.

Tsing, A. L. (2015). *The Mushroom at the End of the World: On the Possibility of Life in Capitalist Ruins*. Princeton: Princeton University Press.

Urry, J. (2005). The complexity turn. *Theory, Culture & Society* 22(5): 1–14.

2 Heterogeneous governance assemblages

Mapping the cases

Introduction: instruments that hold things together and the importance of relations

Throughout history, people have been building and using instruments or apparatuses to govern, control, and discipline others. In the context of contemporary agri-environmental governance (AEG), these instruments can take many guises. They can manifest as regulatory decisions, scientific documents, organisations, or even technology, machinery, and crops. Actors such as governments, agencies, NGOs, and diverse organisations typically build these instruments in the expectation that other actors—often farmers, businesses, or consumers—will follow through and behave in ways that align with certain goals. It is often difficult to judge what the original fundamental intention was behind an instrument. Generally, instruments emerge from a diversity of intentions and motivations that shape the governance assemblage around them. These instruments can have different geographical scopes, from international programmes to local actions, depending on the actors involved in their development. They also vary in terms of the approaches and logics they rely on: regulatory frameworks, financial incentives, knowledge building, and accountability schemes, to name a few. The three cases that we discuss throughout the chapters in this book—IP-Suisse in Switzerland, the Donau Soja project in the European Union, and the Environmental Management and Protection Plan (RPPLH) in Indonesia—are assembled around such instruments.

However, despite narratives and visions of how they will address specific agri-environmental issues, we have found that these instruments unfold something deep and rhizomatic. They open up

DOI: 10.4324/9781003271260-2

complex relationships that were previously hidden or unmanifested, and bring a heterogeneity of actors—human and non-human—in an interweaving of assemblages, leading to continuous negotiations, conflicts, and dynamics between actors. Instruments and apparatuses are key elements of a Foucauldian view of governance. Here, we shift our lens to a Deleuzian view—one that looks at governance as an effect of heterogeneous elements that are constantly negotiating, so much so that it is something that is always becoming—being both ephemeral and, at the same time, sedentary—and whose effects are often uncertain and unpredictable. We therefore pose a critical question in relation to each of our cases in response to the AEG practised in these cases: what will happen if we look at instruments through the lens of assemblage?

In exploring the three cases, this chapter looks at the diversity of "framings" of AEG, mapping the aims and scope of each case in relation to environmental issues in the countries/regions concerned. We underline first that the three cases should not be seen as representing any categorisation of AEG, and they stand on their own as unique case studies amidst the diversity of AEG practices in different parts of the world. They do, however, share a common thread in the sense that what holds them together gravitates around different manifestations of environmental crises that actors in the three cases try to address. These crises provoked the actors into reacting, which then led to the introduction of new elements, approaches, or instruments in the ways they practised AEG. These instruments, as we later illustrate, work in unprecedented ways and unravel new relationships involving wider, heterogeneous, actors. This is what we refer to as heterogeneous governance assemblages, and aforementioned is how the description of each assemblage unfolds.

An assemblage is not any grouping together of things, and it is not a static apparatus and neither is it a map that represents a territory. Assemblage is more a verb than it is a noun, and more like the grammar that creates a language. Assemblage thinking pays careful attention to how things are related, to connections, but more importantly, it concentrates on various dynamics and processes that traverse the social. Assemblage thinking emphasises the constant efforts needed to make assemblages exist, evolve, or dissolve. Deleuze and Guattari use a rich vocabulary to underline the ever-changing character of assemblages. In particular, metaphors such as "molar lines", "molecular lines", and "lines of flight" serve their intention to evidence processes of composition (as well as decomposition) of assemblages and the dynamic interactions with the various elements at play. "Unlike a point, lines are always an articulation, bisection, boundary or breach of a wider field. They are compositional, implying relation and connection" (Windsor, 2015: 157). Indeed, Deleuze refers to molar lines as relations and sees them as defining assemblages in so far as these hold elements together. Molecular lines refer to those processes which allow assemblages to adapt and change. Lines of flight support processes of change but they act in a more transformative and radical manner.

In this first section we introduce our case studies and examples of AEG, starting from the molar—what makes the assemblage cohere. We do so by organising the complex sets of actors we met during our fieldwork around specific instruments of governance. Thus, we start by delineating the assemblages we will explore in this book. We do this by highlighting how these assemblages came to be and progressively formed around a farmer-led certification scheme, a network of public actors committed to European soya production, and a state-led environmental policy.

IP-Suisse: a certification scheme to empower farmers?

IP-Suisse is an abbreviation that refers to a type of agricultural approach—integrated production—and to a country—Switzerland. This name was chosen by a group of farmers in the Canton of Bern, who in 1989 founded a new association with the objective of creating a label for environmentally friendly food production in Switzerland. The IP-Suisse standard first developed around the notion of "integrated production", which aims at reintegrating natural processes in agricultural production, but in a more flexible way than the organic model. Integrated production is defined and standardised by Swiss law, and also inspired the environmental framing of the new agricultural policy at the end of the 1990s. Concretely, an "integrated production" approach seeks to balance production and economic goals with environmental aspects, notably in the use of chemicals (i.e. integrated pest management). IP-Suisse also focused its actions and communications around the promotion of biodiversity on farms, a choice reflected in its logo, a red ladybird. In 2010, IP-Suisse implemented a system based on "biodiversity points" whose goal was to make the contributions to biodiversity on farms clearer—to farmers themselves as well as consumers (Birrer et al., 2014). This point system was developed in collaboration with the Swiss Ornithological Institute (a non-profit foundation supported by the public). In order to accumulate points, IP-Suisse farmers have to implement specific practices that foster biodiversity on their farms, such as building habitats for small animals (e.g. piles of stones, hedges); sowing old varieties (e.g. old breeds of potatoes); maintaining strips of flowery meadows between crops; etc. Another level of requirements is related to specific products that come under this label. Specifications vary from one product to another. For animal products, they mostly focus on animal welfare aspects and feeding systems (e.g. grass-based dairy production). For crops, they generally limit the use of pesticides, growth regulators, and other chemicals. The strength of this limitation varies according to the type of crop, more vulnerable crops such as rapeseed, beetroot, or potatoes being allowed more interventions than others that are less sensitive to pests or disease. In 1993, the first products bearing the IP-Suisse label were sold on the market. Today, the organisation gathers around 18,500 farmer members (out of a total of around 48,000 Swiss farms). IP-Suisse offers an alternative between conventional and organic types of production, which attracted several actors in the Swiss food system. As an illustration, around one-third of the Swiss grain used for baking is IP-Suisse certified.

This first introduction to IP-Suisse as a rather successful instrument of AEG governance, both in terms of farmer participation and market share, is a fairly classical reflection of the model of a tripartite certification scheme (Fouilleux & Loconto, 2017). IP-Suisse is thus not only a farmers' organisation but also a standard for agricultural production and a label used on packaging. The certification is provided by a third-party actor, ProCert, which itself is accredited. Obviously, the birth and development of IP-Suisse are also part of the wider transformation of the Swiss agri-food system. The farmer organisation's standard and practices evolved in constant interaction with other governance practices and instruments led by the state, industries, and retailers. In this sense, it participated in and contributed to a reorganisation and rearticulation of the governance of agriculture, and at the same time was shaped by this broader emerging AEG assemblage.

Donau Soja: a network for rethinking soybeans?

Donau Soja (DS) is a multi-actor organisation with its headquarters in Vienna, Austria. It was founded by a small group of like-minded friends from across the agricultural soya bean sector (including farming associations, seed companies, businesses, etc.). It was established in 2012 with the main goal of promoting the cultivation of soya beans in European regions that are favourable to it, such as the Danube river basin where soya was cultivated in much greater quantities in the past. This was seen as a way to contribute to the overarching goal of furthering the sustainable development of the European food system by reducing the dependency on supplies from other continents, alongside reducing the environmental impacts of a range of agricultural practices which excluded a number of soya's qualities. In designing the DS standard and certification as prime instruments in support of economic–ecological goals, DS also made visible numerous and versatile characteristics of this plant.

Soya beans are used as a legume crop in rotation with wheat or corn to support the fertility of soils; they serve as a cover crop to fix nitrogen in the ground; they are used as feed for livestock because of their rich protein content; and the oil extracted from soya beans is used by industries in a variety of food products. Throughout history, the fascination with the versatile characteristics of this crop kept growing, such that today, Europe is using 40 million tons each year to feed its pigs, fish, chicken, and cattle. Europe is the second-largest importer of soya after China and relies on up to 94% of its supplies coming from the United States, Argentina, and Brazil. Numbers alone show their staggering growth: in terms of production volume, land use, and international trade, soya is among the most important crops in the world today. Over the past 60 years, soya-bean production has increased by almost 1,000% (Oliveira & Schneider, 2016; WWF, 2016), while the area of land cultivated with soya has more than quadrupled (FAOSTAT, n.d.; USDA, 2014). Globally, soya farms now cover 1 million km²—equivalent to the total area of France, Germany, Belgium, and the Netherlands combined (WWF, 2016). In 2013, the world harvest amounted to 284 million tons gathered from 113 million ha (Profundo, 2015). Yet, such expansion has also produced massive overflows and, over the last two decades, businesses, farmers, and representatives of civil society have gradually become aware of the consequences of unlimited growth.

The group of 20 minds that came together to form the DS organisation saw a range of possibilities for breaking with such destructive trajectories. Matthias Krön recalled the history of soya beans in Europe and the time when its cultivation was much more widespread in several European regions, and crop rotation much more present in agricultural practices than today. Indeed, his friend Rudolf Bühler, a pig farmer and founder of the rare-pig-breeds initiative and the farmers' association in Schwäbisch Hall, Germany, showed him how his business managed to rely only on non-genetically modified soya supplies from Serbia. Thus, evidence kept calling for the right moment for the roots of soya beans in Europe to be unearthed. Experts in sustainable certification joined the group to reclaim the possibility of designing a standard for soya beans produced for the Danube river basin that was free from genetic modification, abided by strict land-use-change rules, banned the use of a number of herbicides for desiccation, and furthered fair labour conditions.

DS pioneers succeeded in enrolling an impressive number of the very diverse actors involved in the long value chain of soya beans all across Europe and beyond: from seed production to retailers, from ministries of agriculture to farmers, from multinational agro-industries to research institutes. The diverse range of actors reflected efforts to design the infrastructural setup upon which new value chains could be built in ways that could enable the sustained uptake of soya bean cultivation in Europe.

However, in the case of DS, the process of unlocking the conventional, well-trodden circuits of "increasing returns" (Arthur, 1989) and delusional unlimited extraction has been a bumpy road. Path-dependent processes created difficult conditions for change to break through and assert itself. Yet, the socio-material traits of the crop have turned out to play a central role in steering the course the assemblage takes. Indeed, DS has set itself the goal to integrate the many benefits of soya into the emerging eco-ecological market infrastructures in Europe. There are a number of elements that work in favour of soya with a European origin and for European uses.

RPPLH: a top-down instrument to fix the governance of the environment?

Indonesia's Environmental Management and Protection Plan (*Rencana Pengelolaan dan Perlindungan Lingkungan Hidup* in *Bahasa Indonesia*, or RPPLH for short) is an instrument that helps to address the incongruences of Indonesia's environmental governance. First introduced through the Environmental Management and Protection Act in 2009 (UU 32/2009), RPPLH is an ambitious government project to formulate an all-encompassing environmental management plan that subsumes all other forms of national and regional plans, including the widely referenced medium-term development plans (RPJM) and regional spatial plans (RTRW), both of which serve as the foundations on which the government's various development programmes and projects are established. The enactment of RPPLH also underpins the Indonesian government's novel approach to the way in which business permits are issued. Put simply, every project proposal that poses a potential impact on the environment, be it public- or private-based, must be run through and assessed in reference to guidelines provided by RPPLH. This is a radical change to how environmental planning has often been conducted as, decades ago, a project proposal needed only a case-by-case assessment through what is commonly known as an Environmental Impact Assessment (EIA).

The establishment of RPPLH has been considered a breakthrough because it provides a more integrated approach to environmental governance in Indonesia. It offers a presumably better alternative to the partial, fragmented, and reactive EIA, which often leads to conflicting and overlapping land-use plans. To illustrate, it is not uncommon for an industrial development project that has passed an EIA and been given a project permit to, in fact, conflict with a plan to make use of the land as a strategic agricultural region or conservation forest. Comprehensive environmental planning, such as the one that RPPLH seeks to offer, would avoid that kind of conflict because, in theory at least, a region has first been assigned a function (as an agricultural, industrial, housing, mining, or conservation area, among others) based on its ecological, social, and economic characteristics. In a nutshell, a layperson would read an RPPLH document and find the environmental properties of a single region (based on overlaid data, such as land cover, water capacity, type of soil, climate, population) and the purpose for which the region should be designated in order to maintain the ecological balance whilst serving a wider economic goal.

Currently, central and regional governments are developing their own RPPLHs. For the central government, the term is RPPLHN or *national* environmental protection and management plan, which covers broad-based planning for all the regions of Indonesia. It is intended as a general guideline for provinces and regencies to develop their regional-level RPPLH (or RPPLHD, where D stands for *Daerah*, which literally means "region"). The Ministry of Environment and Forestry is the one responsible for coordinating these plans and providing technical assistance to the provincial and regional governments in formulating well-rounded and scientifically rigorous RPPLHs. Regional governments are developing RPPLHs at different paces and the quality of their planning arguably varies too, although the central government has made serious efforts to ensure that quality standards for RPPLH are met—workshops, technical assistance, and stringent validation processes are among prominent strategies to achieve this.

How RPPLH has unfolded as an imaginary of environmental governance in Indonesia, and the many ways in which it gives rise to a new set of relationships, can be understood if one sees this not as a singular government project in which success is set in opposition to failure but rather as a complex assemblage of heterogeneous elements subject to diverse and sometimes antagonist forces.

Beyond isolated instruments: unfolding wider assemblages

The initial introduction of the three instruments around which we developed our analysis of everyday governance opens new lines of inquiry, new questions, and points to connections with other instruments and practices. The everyday perspective we adopt and its focus on the direct and lived experience of actors involved in governance mean looking beyond the instrument itself, which never exists in isolation and always participates in a broader governance assemblage. From this perspective, new AEG instruments, when introduced, lead to the articulation of new sets of relationships, in other words, the emergence of new governance assemblages. Moreover, paying attention to the interactions between governance instruments and practices is of crucial importance to understanding not only the broader context in which an instrument unfolds but also, and crucially, how practices of governance are reciprocally influencing each other. Rather than situating an instrument in its governance context, the aim is to understand how governance as an assemblage is continuously emerging from the interaction between various governance practices, which in turn are being reshaped through these interactions with the broader governance assemblage.

In the following section, we resituate IP-Suisse, DS, and RPPLH as specific instruments within broader governance assemblages. Doing so means, on the one hand, emphasising the spatialities and temporalities that have provided the conditions for their emergence, and, on the other hand, showing the long chain of self-reinforcing mechanisms that have shaped their development. Indeed, in order to fully understand how these assemblages unfold, we ought to look at how they emerged and shaped the configuration of actors. Looking back and retelling, from an assemblage perspective, the history of these three governance instruments requires us to move away from linear explanations and embrace the multiplicity of the narratives and processes that accompany them across time. We are thus interested in the dynamics between the various elements that take part in the development of specific organisations, specific instruments, and particular crops because these underscore the fundamental dynamic nature of assemblages, namely, that change is the norm rather than the exception. In other words, we want to move away from a linear, fixed, and stable ontology of governance, illustrating what a governance assemblage can be and how it looks in each of our case studies. This endeavour will allow us to exemplify three main features of assemblages, namely: the processes of change and the concept of lines of flight; the continuity in spite of change related to path dependencies and lock-ins; and the internal tensions between antagonist forces.

Lines of flight and the reterritorialisation of AEG assemblages

In the second half of the twentieth century, the combination of instruments supporting production maximisation and market control dominated AEG practices in Switzerland, as it did in most of the Global North. These guiding principles however met with resistance from key elements of broad AEG assemblages. First, the intensification of agricultural production forced important but largely ignored non-human elements—water, soil, biological life, carbon, and nitrogen, to name a few—out of their own ecological trajectories. Second, the global flows of agricultural products stimulated by flows of money (subsidies) and circulation channels based on unequal power relations had a highly destructuring impact on agricultural economies and food politics around the globe. These fundamental tensions within AEG assemblages created fractures and instability. In other words, they drew traversing *lines of flight*[1] that initiated a transformation of the elementary social and biophysical basis of agriculture and life on Earth. Those lines worked together to transform the Swiss AEG assemblage and reconfigure political alliances and priorities along logics of controlling the environmental dimension on the one hand, and a progressive market deregulation on the other. Thus, the Swiss agricultural policy discarded production subsidies to replace them with instruments that would supposedly produce fewer economic disturbances. Direct payments to farmers conditioned on compliance with environmental good practices became a key element in the governance of agriculture. Simultaneously, new traceability instruments emerged from a close collaboration between public and private actors. Standards and certification presented themselves as promising tools to regain control over disruptive non-human elements, for instance the prion causing bovine spongiform encephalopathy. This microscopic entity offers a good example of the central role of non-human elements in the transformation of governance. The prion started to run wild in the 1990s, destabilising agricultural production and raising suspicion and fears among consumers. The response was drastic, with the killing of thousands of animals, the regulation of feed practices, and the development of strict traceability of animals under the control of the state. Finally, the progressive disengagement of the federal state from market and value-chain coordination provoked a deep reorganisation of AEG assemblages, allowing some actors to endorse new levels of responsibility and positions of power. Among other examples, the certification and label system implemented by coalitions of private actors, notably producer organisations and big retailers, started to blossom. The emergence of IP-Suisse as a farmer organisation, a label, and a governance practice was fully embedded in this reterritorialisation of a wider AEG assemblage.

As becomes apparent in this general presentation, the processes of transformation of the AEG assemblage in Switzerland followed multiple and diverse logics and lines of flights. This is not peculiar. As Ong and Collier (2005: 12) put it: "an assemblage is the product of multiple determinations that are not reducible to a single logic". This non-linear, rhizomatic nature of assemblages is also reflected in the way elements engage within the assemblage. Assemblages are not organised along a master plan or a unified project. Even in the cases where a group of actors assembles around a shared objective, multiple expectations and divergent understandings of this objective coexist. Moreover, this core group of human actors needs to enrol other human or non-human elements, which will bring in their own motives. Anna Tsing (2015: 132) describes this ontological multiplicity of agendas well: "Participants come with varied agendas, which do their small part in guiding world-making projects". With this short but insightful comment she also points to the contribution of each element to the making of the assemblage as a whole, to its continuous recreation and reterritorialisation.

The group of farmers who founded IP-Suisse in 1989 had understood the dramatic change that lay ahead of Swiss agriculture. They grasped the emerging trend for a greener and market-oriented governance of food production that started to take shape both in international and national discussions. Anticipating radical changes in the national agricultural policy, they had chosen not to resist, but to try to make the best of a challenging situation by creating a tool that would allow them to get paid for their commitment to more sustainable farm practices. In addition, the aim was to create a platform to nurture the required adaptation of both the structures of the value chains and the competences of the extension and advising institutions. On this basis, and following the tripartite certification model (Loconto & Fouilleux, 2017), this new organisation needed to find allies in order to set up a standard and a control system. A major step was reached in 1997 with the partnership with Migros, one of the two major retail groups in the country. Migros foresaw its own interests in an emerging demand for environment-friendly products in as early as the 1970s and the retailer developed its own M-Sano standard many years before this partnership. Close to the approach chosen by IP-Suisse, this standard supported the principles of integrated production as a model for sustainable agriculture (Bocquet, 2013), and focused on reducing the use of chemicals and improving animal welfare. In the M-Sano system, Migros controlled the standard as well as the whole value chain. By entering into partnership with IP-Suisse, Migros changed its strategy, delegating the definition of the standard and its management to an external partner, IP-Suisse, as a farmer organisation. To understand this strategic U-turn, one can look at Migros's main competitor, the retailer Coop, which engaged in a partnership with the organic food label Biosuisse in 1993. In parallel, the federal state decided to regulate the definition of organic farming. The Ordinance on organic farming came into force on 1 January 1998. These moves by other actors within the AEG assemblage exerted clear pressure on Migros's self-defined environmental standards, which appeared weaker in the new competition on the market for environment-friendly products. At the same time, by referring to integrated production, both Migros and IP-Suisse found an alternative strategy and carved a third way between conventional and organic types of agriculture, as the latter had gained some support and visibility as an agricultural countermodel in the past decades.

As essential intermediaries in the value chain, food processors saw other benefits in joining the assemblage, notably in the coordination capacity offered by this new set of relations between partners within the certification scheme. The industrial baker Jowa and the grain industry offer a good illustration of how the implementation of a tripartite certification scheme such as IP-Suisse is supported by parallel needs. Before the major reforms undergone by the agricultural policy, the federal state used to coordinate and control the Swiss production of grain in terms of both quantity and quality. The state's withdrawal from market control created an urgent need for an alternative way of coordinating the quantity as well as quality of grain and flour provisioning. With its direct access to farmers and cross-cutting dimension, the IP-Suisse assemblage offered a welcome potential to develop new ways of coordinating supply and demand in the value chain.

Path-dependent processes and lock-ins

Efforts to reassemble soya in the European imagination and European agricultural cultivation practice are intimately tied to the recent history of soya beans and their global career after World War II. The dominant use of this crop in economies of scale over the last seven decades has entangled soya into a web of material and symbolic relations which are proving hard to break out from. Indeed, stabilising territorialisation forces and lines of flight—or deterritorialisation forces—collide and compete in spacetimes where soya's value is reclaimed in multiple ways.

Dominant understandings of soya as a cheap protein produced far away to feed Europe's animal industry efficiently began to crumble at the dawn of the twenty-first century. Non-linear understandings of the indirect and unintended consequences of past actions among scientific, political, and civil actors have begun to fuel the need for new narratives that rethink productivist models of agricultural governance. The largely unintended and overlooked consequences of the ubiquitous and exponential use of soya amount to biodiversity loss, deforestation, land grabs, environmental pollution, and intensive monoculture agriculture.

A constellation of political agreements and technological developments transformed soya into a lucrative pursuit for producing and consuming countries alike. The Blair House Agreement of the Uruguay Round in the early 1990s exempted soya beans from import tariffs imposed on other major crops such as wheat or maize. This decision enabled a chain of reactions that in time led to a gradual decrease in the cultivation of soya beans and legumes in Europe from 4% to less than 2% of land devoted to this crop in the late 2000s. This in turn led to a European specialisation in wheat, with investment and research increasingly flowing in its favour, and to the marginalisation of legumes (Magrini et al., 2016). This path was further reinforced with the advent of biotechnologies and the introduction, in 1994, of the Roundup Ready soya bean, the first genetically modified plant in the United States, also authorised for cultivation in Argentina and Brazil a few years later. Despite consumers' resistance in Europe, genetically modified soya beans benefited from the European Union's coexist-ence policy (see Reynolds & Szerszynski, 2014) and rapidly sneaked through the back door of market regulation as an "embedded" food ingredient and feed compound. Today, 90% of soya beans imported in Europe are genetically modified.

The vocal reports (e.g. Profundo, 2015) released by NGOs in the first decade of the 2000s, exposing the dark side of soya's success, provided wake-up calls for many concerned actors in Europe. Switzerland was among the first countries to act. Fully embracing the non-GMO (gen-etically modified organisms) consensus, the country's two dominant retailers developed action plans to promote sustainable soya bean imports. The result was the establishment of the Basler Criteria for Sustainable Soy guidelines (2004), which were to become a defining benchmark not only for the national but also the international creation of standards for soya beans. Those guidelines place deforestation- and land-conversion-free soya as fundamental requirements, which were also endorsed in the DS standard. Subsequent agreements and declar-ations came to strengthen these, such as the Brussels Soy Declaration (2012) whereby European soya industries support the non-GM (gen-etically modified) cultivation of soya beans in Brazil, the Roundtable for Sustainable Soy (2006), and the Berlin Declaration for a GMO-free Europe (2018). These different yet interrelated developments provided some solid anchoring points and a good degree of impetus for DS to launch its programmes.

This short history of soya explains the political and economic conditions in which Europe's animal farming and meat industry gained traction and grew exponentially. Entrenched beliefs and practices as to the profitability of meat in the Global North and of soya in the Global South have established paths that are hard to reverse or reform. Flows of finance support research on grain in Europe, flows of overseas soya sustain the freight industries, and flows of convenient nitrogen fertilisers feed soils in Europe, rendering nitrogen-fixing crops unattractive. Nowadays, Europe is still dependent on up to 94% of imported soya beans. The lack of adequate alternative sources of protein to feed the millions of chickens and pigs raised in highly concentrated and industrialised production units create a lock-in situation compared to which all the efforts deployed by NGOs and other actors seem minor or even futile.

Internal tensions and centralisation forces

In order to comprehend why a seemingly simple instrument such as RPPLH could gain enough traction from multiple stakeholders, we need to understand how environmental issues in Indonesia were hidden in the background amidst the drive towards the Green Revolution in the 1970s and its ensuing industrialisation in the 1980s. During that period, many environmental problems ensued in Indonesia's endeavours towards development. Pest outbreaks and soil degradation in most of the arable lands in Java only became obvious in the 1990s, along with ENSO-related droughts and floods (Dwiartama, 2014). Rapid deforestation has occurred steadily since the massive opening up of Indonesia's natural forest to the timber industry in the 1970s (Tsing, 2005; Peluso, 1988), only to be followed by the rapid expansion of oil palm plantations in the 2000s (McCarthy, 2012). Environmental degradation has, however, been mostly felt in Java, the country's most populous island, as industry has started to take its toll on the watersheds and local residents across the island.

The instability and ephemerality of Indonesia's environmental governance have been the subject of many social studies highlighting the incongruences, dissonance, and friction among actors in the assemblage (Li, 2007; Tsing, 2005; Dwiartama et al., 2016; Dwiartama, 2018). This offers a counternarrative of fragility in governance assemblages which lies in contrast with the examples of progressive and continuous processes of change or rigid and enduring configurations provided by the other two case studies, IP-Suisse and DS. The story begins with Indonesia's notable Environment Act, which was first enacted in 1982—a simple document, merely seven pages long, which lays out every citizen's rights to a clean environment and their responsibility to take care of their environment for the sake of everyone. As the environmental crisis grew more complex, Indonesia's Ministry of Environment pushed for the enactment of a more comprehensive Environment Management Act in 1997. This new law detailed the role of the government to set environmental quality standards and thresholds, as well as obliged citizens to comply with those standards in every form of activity, including business. This was followed by the Environmental Management and Protection Act in 2009, which mandated the central government, as well as the provincial and regional governments, to develop environmental management and monitoring plans that may provide strict guidelines and avenues for development, land-use planning, and business activities.

This mandate complements the existing regulations on environmental impact assessment (*Analisis Mengenai Dampak Lingkungan*, AMDAL), with which every form of business and economic activity—industry, construction, mining, forestry, and agriculture—must comply and put together a predevelopment plan to ensure that environmental impacts and risks are assessed and anticipated. AMDAL/EIA puts an emphasis on comprehensive data collection of environmental indicators, which broadly consist of biodiversity, soil, water, and air quality, as well as the socio-economic profile of the locale in which a project is expected to proceed. This is a process which requires not only the business entities but also consultants, local community groups, environmental activists, and local governments to agree upon the acceptable limit of the potential impact of the said project. In many cases, the tentative assemblage of all these humans as well as non-humans (water, plants, animals, microbes, heavy metals, soil, and others) does not seem to hold together: business actors fail to comply with the regulations; environmental data do not show any positive impact on the environment; local communities clash with environmental activists due to the perceived risks and benefits of the project; etc. The many differing, or even conflicting, interests, desires, and perspectives, in other words, too many internal tensions and lines of flight and too few binding and attracting forces—dissolve the assemblage before it can be territorialised.

It is due to this situation that the government is proposing a new logic to its environmental planning and policies. Instead of relying on localised data collection and risk assessment to respond to a certain development project, the national government—with the support and collaboration of each of the 31 provincial governments and hundreds of regional governments—would have to devise an encompassing environmental management and monitoring plan that highlights what sort of development project should and should not be implemented in a particular place. An environmental assessment and planning document, titled the National/Regional Environmental Management and Monitoring Plan (RPPLH-N/D), would become the preferred document, surpassing any other planning documents—including the Regional Spatial Plan (RTRW) and Long/Medium-Term Development Plan (RPJP/M)—which prior to this were key references for any regional development project. In short, the government tries to fight deterritorialisation of governance assemblages with centralisation, as a line of articulation.

Governance assemblages as multiplicities

Deleuze and Guatarri (1988: 33) insisted on the importance of thinking multiplicity, which is not the same as the individual or the multiple and opens a new possibility to think beyond this misleading binary opposition. Multiplicities are simultaneously one and many. Assemblages are multiplicities: they are made up of multiple elements with various multiple properties, intentions, and desires, and are traversed by diverging forces. But an assemblage is also one, a productive and creative whole, which is actually defined by what emerges from itself through the interactions of its multiple elements (Buchanan, 2021: 47). In this sense, the individuality of an assemblage is continuously produced and recreated, otherwise the assemblage will be deterritorialised, dissolved. It has to be noted here that, from an assemblage-thinking perspective, the individual and the collective are not a question of scale. As DeLanda puts it:

> As an ontological category the term "individual" has no preference for any one particular level of scale. It is perfectly possible to speak of individual communities, individual organisations, individual cities. Similarly, we can, without invoking any undesirable connotations, speak of individual atoms, individual molecules, individual cells, and individual organs. All of these entities are assemblages, their defining emergent properties produced by their interacting parts, and therefore contingent on the occurrence of the requisite interactions. The historicity and individuality of all

assemblages forces us as materialists to confront the question of the historical processes which produced or brought into being any given assemblage. We may refer to these as *processes of individuation.*

(DeLanda, 2016: 140)

In this sense, assemblage thinking offers a complex and nuanced framing for thinking of the individual and the collective. In this section we engage with the dual nature—one and many—of the governance assemblages we studied, as multiplicities.

Multiplicity as diversity of reasons to assemble

Creating opportunities for premium prices, securing a leading position and good image in retail, reinventing the coordination of the value chain, those are just a few examples of the diverse agenda that motivated actors to engage in the IP-Suisse assemblage. This multiplicity of agendas and motivations combines in the assemblage and helps to constantly produce, reproduce, and transform it. As already shown, the synergies with the environmental schemes under the federal agricultural policy and the marketing strategy of Migros contributed to the success of IP-Suisse. As acknowledged by the actors themselves, most of the actions required by the IP-Suisse standard are also integrated in and rewarded by the federal agricultural policy. For farmers, this produces a double incentive resulting in both flows of public money through the direct payment system and premium prices for their products. Both the state policy and the label become more attractive for farmers, thanks to this complementarity. BioSuisse, the national association for organic farmers, also played an essential if indirect role in the shaping of IP-Suisse, both as a model and a competitor. At the same time, the partnership with a farmers' owned and certified standard was confirmed as the dominant model. Here also, what IP-Suisse became is totally embedded in this reorganisation of markets and economic relations in the food system. The partnership with Migros not only served the retailer, who could claim its commitment to sustainable Swiss food production, it also obviously contributed to the rapid confirmation of IP-Suisse as a leading food label on the Swiss market. Simultaneously, however, retailers have been very active in developing their own sustainability brands and standards, using their strategic position to impose quality standards on their economic partners, notably farmers.

Many other elements contributed to the general evolution of the Swiss agricultural sector, notably actors in the agricultural knowledge system, including extension services, agricultural schools, universities, and research centres. In sum, IP-Suisse emerged and is still developing in a context of deep reterritorialisation of a wider AEG assemblage. What IP-Suisse became and the outcomes of its development—what it produced—cannot be understood correctly if we ignore this embeddedness. And this statement is also valid for any of the aforementioned governance practices that have been developing within this assemblage: each of them is inevitably shaped by its relations with the others, and shapes them in turn. From an assemblage perspective, it makes no sense to look at any of these AEG instruments or practices in isolation. In other words, IP-Suisse as an assemblage emerges from the convergence of these multiple elements and forms a multiplicity. Remove one of them and IP-Suisse would be something else.

Multiplicity as diversity of imaginaries

Given the favourable winds encountered by the initiators of DS, the making of the standard took off quickly. A variety of actors became participants in this endeavour. Within a few years, it developed into a transnational poly-centred network of like-minded agricultural experts where each regional or national chapter is steered by consultants, researchers, or business people from 25 countries. DS has 316 members including civil-society bodies, businesses and entrepreneurs, governmental and non-governmental organisations, and members from most of the sectors of the value chain, such as seed-breeding companies, soya producers, traders, soya bean processors, feed and food industries, and many of the largest retail companies in Europe. This heterogeneity of actors reflects the long and complex value chain of soya. The socio-material relations forming around soya came to reveal a multitude of interrelations between the various stages of production and processing and, as such, also a range of possible points of intervention in the soya market.

The spatial arrangement of the soya bean crop across Europe and the distinctive elements included in the standard, certification, and labelling system brought to light a series of related tensions that DS confronted head-on. It started with the awareness that the operation of the standard and the certification was closely linked to the availability of seeds of levels of quality that differed from those in the dominant market. This sparked the search for public and private seed-breeding research and development institutions across Europe devoted to non-GM markets. It also led to a careful strengthening of relations with the largest non-GM seed bank in China—as the cradle of soya beans—and the setting up of partnerships (agreements of understanding) with the Chinese Academy of Sciences, meant to safeguard the variety of seeds as a basis for biodiverse ecosystems. Thus, the development and implementation of the standard proved to be a constantly growing field not only of facts but also of concerns, resulting in new relations that have expanded the assemblage across values chains and geographical boundaries.

The socio-technical possibilities afforded by the instrument led DS to engage in growing the network of actors in a variety of domains and locales dedicated to promoting certain qualities of soya. But socio-technical possibilities rarely play out in a linear and predictable manner. As different groups of actors enter the governance arena, distinct social imaginaries of soya's value for Europe come to be articulated and these do not always converge in a single vision for soya. As a result, DS is confronting and engaging with different—often clashing—imaginaries of soya and, consequently, with diverse visions of what DS should do and become. Each of these imaginaries and visions would, by itself, lead the whole assemblage towards a different future. As long as the assemblage coheres, though, they all work together and set a direction that results from this diversity.

Pálsson and Rabinow (2005: 94) highlight the role of assemblage as a concept that enables us to understand "a specific historical, political, and economic conjuncture in which an issue becomes a problem". The interplay of the diverse social imaginaries of soya is thus framing the construction of concerns and the identification of problems within the DS assemblage. This internal discussion on matters of concern (Latour, 2004) lays the ground on which the potential to transform, reconfigure, or disrupt wider assemblages to which DS is connected can emerge. In the process of building the standard, soya has turned into a network of relations that go well beyond the boundaries of a technical and agronomic problem. DS's concern with the infrastructural elements of soya and the interdependent relations that make up its circulation and use shows that a variety of responses is necessary in order to enable the desired transformation not just of the cultivation and circulation of one crop, but of the food systems that the crop is part of. The organisation does more than build and mobilise a complex set of actions and understandings, it equally raises very high stakes in respect to politics, the environment, and the economy. The stakes are high because aims and actions involve changing policies on issues—notably the dependency on imported protein—that have not been addressed over the past 40 years. In addition, they respond to imperatives of change posed by the looming climate crisis in relation to the production of soya on deforested land and a still-growing global meat industry, and therefore they confront dominant markets. Last but not least, and maybe more fundamentally, these stakes involve revisiting a set of engrained beliefs and understandings around this one specific crop that is soya.

Multiplicity as a messy process

RPPLH is a grandiose yet bureaucratic-utopian project. For one thing, it is built on the basis of a comprehensive set of data that no regional government has ever successfully compiled. On paper, the idea of RPPLH is relatively straightforward: governments need to overlay different forms of spatial data upon their territories, be they land use, land cover, climate, water potential, flow and use, geological data, soil types, ecosystem types, forest cover, biodiversity, oil/coal/mineral deposits below ground, agricultural/forestry/livestock/fishery potential, waste production, population density, demography, economic activities, health facilities, cultural diversity, and basically anything that can be digitised and superimposed on a map. Data will be populated by different sectoral offices and agencies. So, for example, the Forestry Agency will be responsible for collecting and reporting on forest cover, type, and potential. The Agricultural Agency will then fill in the regional agricultural production (arable land, soil type, land suitability, crops grown, productivity, and many other variables). The Regional Planning Agency is in charge of coordinating this data collection with more than 20 agencies and offices to provide a rather complete set of spatial data for the RPPLH. These overlays of spatial data are then interpreted and translated into scores by first weighting each of the datasets. Experts will mainly be called in to make such judgements. After the weight of each set of data is agreed on, its score is established on a specific spatial grid, and a distribution of colour-coded grids shows what sort of development project can and cannot be carried out in a specific area or region.

In practice and from an everyday perspective, however, the RPPLH instrument is the epitome of far more messy and complex processes.

The document brings together different government agencies and sectors in ways that have never been tried before. Each RPPLH—there is one national RPPLHN and many more provincial and regional RPPLHDs—is formulated by a working group, most often led by the Regional/National Planning Agency, but in some provinces and regions the Environmental Agency plays much of this role. A consultant is usually present to gather and analyse data, but the working group has a more active role in deciding the type of strategies to be implemented for a given set of data. Discussions have never been easy. Each office attempts to influence the spatial configuration of data, to ensure that its own data is the one that speaks the loudest in the layering of information on a map. To illustrate, the settlement office would bring population data to the table and argue that the need for housing should be given more weight in an area's development priorities. The Agricultural Agency would then counterargue that the area is instead better suited for food production, considering the soil quality, water availability, and food demand in the surrounding area. Negotiations and decisions on spatial planning have become more complicated. Prior to RPPLH, decisions were mostly made by the Planning Agency on the basis of what the president, governor, or regent aimed to achieve over the next five to ten years. With RPPLH, the materiality and subjectivity of data play a more central role in providing guidance on how development needs to be planned out. In other words, the instrument fundamentally changes the internal politics of planning.

The process of formulating RPPLH can take longer than expected because of this situation. It is not uncommon for the leadership role to shift from one agency to another due to unresolved conflicting interests. Lines of articulation—efforts to bring all together—are most often accompanied by lines of flight—disagreement among government agencies that stall the formulation of the environmental management and protection plans. Disagreement on how to proceed with the structure of the document and standard means of analysis has left even the Ministry of Environment and Forestry—the very body responsible for putting together a standardised RPPLH document—befuddled. In some cases where a province or regency has successfully drawn up a complete document and all agencies have agreed upon its content, other actors such as legislatures, businesses, NGOs, and community representatives will also have to support the plan in order for RPPLH to play out as an instrument that really holds things together. Since

RPPLH became a legal instrument in 2009, there has been no province or regency that truly implements its development plans on the basis of this document due to the dynamics occurring within this complex set of assemblages.

The messy process of negotiating an assemblage like RPPLH cannot be separated from the messiness of data itself. Data, at least in the case of RPPLH, has gone beyond a mere part of an instrument. It is in itself a complex and messy assemblage. To borrow Latour's idea of a black box, data is singular (in the sense that everyone talks about "the data" in reference to the scientific bundle of numbers and figures to be used as the basis of environmental planning), but at the same time plural and multiple (in that it is composed of still-life portraits of various phenomena, each representing a "dividual" aspect of reality; see Deleuze, 1995). How data is understood as an abstract materiality (Kitchin, 2014), which is perceived, engaged with, and politicised differently by different actors, has led to data being more than just a "bundle of figures". It too has become a (non-human) actor that territorialises in a way that brings a certain dynamic to the wider assemblage. The effectiveness of RPPLH as an instrument to hold certain actors together (or break them apart) depends on the configuration of data as a multiplicity and how one part speaks to another. Data on population density, when superimposed with waste-production data, brings different results to the assemblage as compared to when it is linked to food production. In what way should the human actors then make use of the data? It seems that there is no certainty as to who owns, collects, and nurtures data, and how data is meaningful to one but not another. Data in general, but particularly in the context of RPPLH, adds a sort of messiness to the assemblage that leads an environmental management plan to never truly take shape—it is always becoming, and one added set of data always creates a new version of RPPLH and the wider assemblage associated with it. This messiness of data thus translates into the messiness of the wider assemblage.

Concluding remarks: assemblages highlighting the complex dynamics of governance

In this chapter we have introduced the reader to an assemblage approach to AEG. To do so, we have mobilised three contrasting examples of governance instruments that serve as an entry point to broader governance assemblages. IP-Suisse as a certification scheme opens up a complex network of actors across value chains and public policies. Donau Soja, as a standard and certification programme and a wider-reaching plan to rethink agricultural practices in their interrelated workings, expands the range of questions, problems, and solutions beyond the borders of the organisation and the instrument as such. Finally, the Indonesian RPPLH boils down to a data cauldron of seemingly endless possibilities to reorganise environmental planning.

This exploration of the three assemblages has allowed us to highlight key features of assemblage. Assemblages are dynamic because they are traversed by lines of flight that attract the element that constitute them, towards diverging paths and assembling forces, and therefore produce forces of destabilisation or deterritorialisation of the whole. At the same time, forces of cohesion—or lines of articulation—deployed in the assemblage work to hold things together and either perpetuate the current configuration of the assemblage or stabilise new formations in a process of reterritorialisation. Under certain circumstances, assemblages may also be strongly territorialised by forces anchored in the path carved by their progressive evolution. Governance interventions share the same dual nature. In the end, the balance between forces of change and those of stabilisation is at the focus of attention in any assemblage framing.

Another feature of assemblage highlighted through the presentation of our case studies relates to the notion of multiplicity. Assemblages are multiplicities, are one and many at the same time (Deleuze & Guatarri, 1988). This multiplicity is reflected in the diverse motivations and projects that animate the elements joining in the assemblage and the sometimes divergent imaginaries of what could be the future and how to reach it. Assemblages are therefore messy, full of internal tensions and ambiguities. Thinking with assemblages requires "an ethos of engagement that attends to the messiness and complexity of phenomena" (Anderson et al., 2012: 175). Governance practices that might look stable are not what they seem. Acknowledging this messiness leads to a better understanding of what governance is from an everyday perspective. It is also important to build future governance actions that are not based on an illusion of order and control. The value of anticipating messiness lies indeed in the fundamental unpredictability of the outcomes of the governance practices applied on complex issues, such as agri-environmental problems. How to understand this unpredictability and its ramifications in terms of intentionality, desirability, and integration is the subject matter of the next chapter.

Note

1 Deleuze and Guatarri define lines of flight as "movements of deterritorialisation and destratification" (1987: 3). DeLanda offers this complement: "lines of flight, marking the direction in which an assemblage can become deterritorialized" (2016: 109).

References

Anderson, B., Kearnes, M., McFarlane, C., & Swanton, D. (2012). On assemblages and geography. *Dialogues in Human Geography* 2(2): 171–189.

Arthur, W. B. (1989). Competing technologies, increasing returns, and lock-in by historical events. *The Economic Journal* 99(394): 116–131.

Birrer, S., Zellweger-Fischer, J., Stoeckli, S., Korner-Nievergelt, F., Balmer, O., Jenny, M., & Pfiffner, L. (2014). Biodiversity at the farm scale: A novel credit point system. *Agriculture, Ecosystems & Environment* 197: 195–203.

Bocquet, A.-M. (2013). L'engagement environnemental de l'entreprise: quelle responsabilité envers quelles parties prenantes? Les cas Migros et Coop sur le marché agroalimentaire suisse. *Management & Avenir* 64(6): 35–55.

Buchanan, I. (2021). *Assemblage Theory and Method*. London/ New York: Bloomsbury.

DeLanda, M. (2016). *Assemblage Theory*. Edinburgh: Edinburgh University Press.

Deleuze, G. (1995). *Negotiations 1972–1990* (Translated by Martin Joughin). New York: Columbia University Press.

Deleuze, G., & Guatarri, F. (1988). *A Thousand Plateaus: Capitalism and Schizophrenia*. London: Athlone.

Dwiartama, A. (2014). *Investigating Resilience of Agriculture and Food Systems: Insights from Two Theories and Two Case Studies*. Doctoral Dissertation. New Zealand: University of Otago.

Dwiartama, A. (2018). From 'disciplinary societies' to 'societies of control': An historical narrative of agri-environmental governance in Indonesia. In J. Forney, C. Rosin, & H. Campbell (Eds.). *Agri-environmental Governance as an Assemblage: Multiplicity, Power, and Transformation* (pp. 91–104). London and New York: Routledge.

Dwiartama, A., Rosin, C., & Campbell, H. (2016). Understanding agri-food systems as assemblages. In R. Le Heron, H. Campbell, N. Lewis, & M. Carolan (Eds.). *Biological Economies: Experimentation and the Politics of Agri-food Frontiers* (pp. 82–94). London and New York: Routledge.

FAOSTAT (Food and Agriculture Organization Statistics Division). (n.d.). *Crop Production STAT Calculators*. Rome: FAO

Fouilleux, E., & Loconto, A. (2017). Voluntary standards, certification, and accreditation in the global organic agriculture field: a tripartite model of techno-politics. *Agriculture and Human Values* 34(1): 1–14.

Kitchin, R. (2014). Big Data, new epistemologies and paradigm shifts. *Big Data & Society* 1(1): 2053951714528481.

Latour, B. (2004). Why has critique run out of steam? From matters of fact to matters of concern. *Critical Inquiry* 30(2): 225–248.

Li, T. M. (2007). Practices of assemblage and community forest management. *Economy and Society* 36(2): 263–293.

Magrini, M. B., Anton, M., Cholez, C., Corre-Hellou, G., Duc, G., Jeuffroy, M. H., Meynard, J.M., Pelzer, E., Voisin, A. S., & Walrand, S. (2016). Why are grain-legumes rarely present in cropping systems despite their environmental and nutritional benefits? Analyzing lock-in in the French agrifood system. *Ecological Economics* 126: 152–162.

McCarthy, J. F. (2012). Certifying in contested spaces: private regulation in Indonesian forestry and palm oil. *Third World Quarterly* 33(10): 1871–1888.

Oliveira, G., & Schneider, M. (2016). The politics of flexing soybeans: China, Brazil and global agroindustrial restructuring. *The Journal of Peasant Studies*, *43*(1): 167–194.

Ong, A., & Collier, S. J. (Eds.). (2005). *Global Assemblages. Technology, Politics and Ethics as Anthropological Problems*. Malden/Oxford/Victoria: Blackwell Publishing.

Pálsson, G., & Rabinow, P. (2005). The Iceland controversy: reflections on the transnational market of civic virtue. In A. Ong, & S. J. Collier (Eds.). *Global Assemblages. Technology, Politics and Ethics as Anthropological Problems* (pp. 91–103). Malden/Oxford/Victoria: Blackwell Publishing.

Peluso, N. L. (1988). *Rich Forests, Poor People, and Development: Forest Access Control and Resistance in Java*. New York: Cornell University.

Profundo. (2015). *Mapping the Soy Supply Chain in Europe*. A research paper prepared for WNF. www.profundo.nl/page/show/themes/p718#__2015__ p-718. (Accessed 9 July 2017).

Reynolds, L., & Szerszynski, B. (2014). The post-political and the end of nature: the genetically modified organism. In J. Wilson & E. Swyngedouw (Eds.). *The Postpolitical and Its Discontents* (pp. 48–67). Edinburgh: Edinburgh University Press.

Tsing, A. L. (2005). *Friction: An Ethnography of Global Connection*. Princeton: Princeton University Press.

Tsing, A. L. (2015). *The Mushroom at the End of the World: On the Possibility of Life in Capitalist Ruins*. Princeton: Princeton University Press.

Undang-Undang Republik Indonesia No. 32. (2009). Tentang Pengelolaan dan Perlindungan Lingkungan Hidup (*Law on Environmental Management and Protection*).

USDA (United States Department of Agriculture—Foreign Agricultural Service). (2014, July). Oilseeds. World Markets and Trade. https://fas.usda.gov/data/oilseeds-world-markets-and-trade [Accessed on 19 April 2022].

Windsor, J. (2015). Desire lines: Deleuze and Guattari on molar lines, molecular lines, and lines of flight. *New Zealand Sociology* 30(1): 156–171.

WWF (World Wildlife Fund). (2016). *Soy Scorecard: Assessing the Use of Responsible Soy for Animal Feed*. Gland, Switzerland.

3 Unpredictability of effects in agri-environmental governance

Introduction: the unpredictable nature of governance

The heterogeneity of elements and process-making of agri-environmental governance (AEG) assemblages points to their complexity and the difficulties in anticipating the real effects of governance instruments and actions in everyday life. Unexpected and side effects of governance practices are too often overlooked because monitoring developments and progress is usually focused on the assessment of success or failure and their causes. An everyday perspective on AEG, on the contrary, embraces the multiplicity of effects of governance and sees their unpredictability not as a failure or a limitation, but as the result of the inescapable nature of complex assemblages. Unexpected effects are not considered as problems anymore, instead they define what an AEG assemblage actually creates. Indeed, as phrased by Buchanan (2021), assemblages are actually defined by what emerges from them and by what they do.

In this chapter, we highlight the multiplicity of the effects of governance practices in our case studies, with a focus on the unexpected and the unwanted, as well as ways in which actors anticipate and make do with this. In order to do so, we shift attention from the main instruments that are intended to govern, to other ordering devices that shape the course of action. We raise a few fundamental and defining questions: What is being governed? What do the actors aim to solve? Is there any "side effect" from the solution? What else is actually happening? What are the things considered a failure or success? What effects does this failure/success provide? And is there any "new" instrument that people look into, in addition to the main instruments?

DOI: 10.4324/9781003271260-3

The three case studies that we examine in this book exemplify how we question and engage with the effects of governance. A traditional view of governance will commonly start from the explicit objectives of the instruments and mobilise indicators to assess success or failure. In the best cases, a few collateral aspects might be monitored as well. However, how governance practices contribute to the transformation or stabilisation of a broader assemblage is rarely explored. This way of thinking effects and outcomes is linear and follows a logic based on anticipation and expectation. It derives directly from a linear problem-solving conception of governance based on schematisation and simplification, assuming rather simple mechanisms. As Scott (1998: 6) critically points to what he sees as the inescapable failure of this kind of governance: "Designed or planned social order is necessarily schematic; it always ignores essential features of any real, functioning social order", which is always complex and multiple.

Indeed, as history shows, governance practices only rarely reach all—and only—the results announced and expected. The impossibility of predicting the evolution and developments of complex "systems" is repeatedly mentioned in the literature (Capra, 1996; Levin, 1999; Law & Mol, 2002), and particularly in relation to sustainability matters. Many factors mingle and render social–ecological transformation unpredictable: hidden abodes, external interventions, fortuitous interactions and events, as well as diverse forms of resistance (e.g. Voß & Kemp, 2006). Because of these difficulties that are met in achieving explicit goals, Miller and Rose (1990) speak of the idea of "government" as a "congenitally failing operation". Consequently, they claim, the "will to govern" needs to be understood "in terms of the difficulties of operationalising it", as the unruly nature of social life can never be fully captured by any form of knowledge that informs governing programmes (Miller & Rose, 1990: 10–11). Therefore, as Walker and Shove (2007) argue for sustainability, contingencies and ambivalences in the pursuit of governance objectives have to be seen as "a normal rather than a pathological state".

The unpredictable nature of outcomes of policies has been discussed by Voß and Kemp (2006) in relation to the concept of reflexive governance. The authors identify three characteristics of sustainable development that are also valid for AEG:

> … first, the heterogeneity of elements, which precludes relying on disciplinary expert knowledge; second, the impossibility of

predicting system developments and the effects of interventions, which makes errors unavoidable; and third, the irreversibility of social development, which embeds a strong path dependency in decision making.

(Voß & Kemp, 2006: 10)

This also aligns with what James Ferguson asserts in his book, *The Anti-Politics Machine* (1994), on the side effects of the failure of development projects. Although Ferguson mainly criticises the failed attempt to understand the anthropological context that underlies development, he also argues that focusing on the technical aspect of failures is not enough; we should also embrace the complexity and unpredictability of effects of any development project.

We assert that this unpredictability is inherent to the nature of assemblages itself, its heterogeneity, complexity, and emerging nature. This complexity of assemblages builds into discrepancies between stated objectives and outcomes, which are apparent when one adopts an everyday perspective (Forney & Dwiartama, 2023; Bentia, 2021). From this everyday perspective, AEG emerges in the dynamics and tensions between governance actions, anticipation of outcomes, strategies to control them, inevitable overflows of unintended/unexpected outcomes, and the manifestation of new actions.

Here, we need to clarify what we mean by unintended, unpredictable, and unwanted. We refer to philosopher Frank de Zwart (2015), who calls to attention the distinction between unanticipated and unintended consequences, and the fact that sociology has mostly conflated the two concepts. He argues that unintended consequences have largely been used to address the unwelcome effects of policy and this has had the detrimental effect of obscuring the unanticipated outcomes produced by any social action. In this sense, he recalls Alejandro Portes's 1999 presidential address to the American Sociological Association, in which he described sociology as the analysis of the unexpected (thus paying homage to Merton's pioneering research from 1936). In reference to this, we use the concept of the unintended as something that is not part of a planned objective, but can potentially be anticipated and may lead to good outcomes too. Something unwanted, on the other hand, implies negative and undesirable effects. The two merge in the idea of unpredictability, which acts as a starting point for why reflexive actors try to regain as much control as possible.

In addition to this, we then look at assemblages as being more than just unpredictable, resulting also in multiple outcomes. AEG assemblages, in this sense, are traversed by many heterogeneous processes that happen simultaneously. The heterogeneity of assemblages and the multiple effects it produces opens our analysis to a reflection on and assessment of a range of emergent governance processes that emphasises the diversity of possible (governance) outcomes and, connected to this, a questioning and search for "what" (ontology) is being governed.

In the following sections, we look into this unpredictability of effects as it relates to various touching points stemming from our cases. In the case of RPPLH, we look into what we termed "a productive failure", a new trajectory emanating from the ruins of an AEG assemblage. In the case of IP-Suisse, the emphasis is on this multiplicity of intended and unintended processes and outcomes, which opens up new possibilities. In the case of Donau Soja (DS), we highlight the agency of non-human actors in creating multiple pathways within the assemblage and ways in which human actors attempt to anticipate these effects by piggybacking on this unpredictability of effects.

A productive failure emerging from the unpredictable assemblage effect

Messy assemblages that paved the way for a failed governance

In Chapter 2, we highlighted that in the case of RPPLH in Indonesia, a complex set of data has been instrumental in making a new environmental governance assemblage. Data becomes something that is plural (it consists of different forms of data—numerical, categorical, spatial, tabular—and comes from various sources—environmental, agricultural, settlement, transportation, public work, forestry, and others), but also singular (a form of Latourian black box). We illustrated how the complexity of data leads to a complex assemblage of actors.

This chapter further investigates the extent to which this complex assemblage leads to frictions, flights, and reassembling of actors that go beyond what was originally planned (what is deemed as failure). Indeed, as a regulatory and planning document, RPPLH is far from being an accommodative instrument for all whose stakes are at risk, let alone being used effectively as an environmental guideline for development programmes. However, it was through the impasses, confusions, convolutions, intricacies, and, to an extent, conflicts that actors began to weave new relations and connections that resulted in unintended effects, whilst opening up new ways of governance.

West Java, the most populated province in Indonesia, illustrates this point. West Java Provincial Government, or to be precise, its Environmental Agency, has been mandated by the governor to lead the development of the province's RPPLHD since 2016. It was among the first provinces to initiate the project. It is also, unfortunately, the one arguably facing the most challenges in running it. At the beginning of the process, the West Java province had already been the subject of various mega-development projects: Southeast Asia's first high-speed railway that will connect two of the largest cities in Java; Jatigede, Indonesia's second-largest hydroelectric dam; West Java's international airport in Majalengka; and a massive network of highways connecting different cities on the island. The Government of Indonesia is also determined to achieve food security by designating hundreds of thousands of hectares of agricultural area on the north coast of West Java as "permanent agricultural regions". This is in contradiction with the ever-growing residential development in the same area due to its proximity to Jakarta, Bekasi, and Cirebon, three of the largest cities on the north coast of Java. All of these conflicting development projects occurred while Jakarta was, and still is, experiencing land subsidence, sea-level rise, and climate-related events threatening agricultural production in those strategic regions; erosions, landslides, and river pollution are happening in almost all large river basins; and air quality is at its worst, particularly in the cities of Jakarta, Bekasi, Bandung, and Cirebon.

This illustration should provide a good-enough context to how "wicked" the environmental conditions in West Java really are. When the Environmental Agency took a lead in complying with the national mandate to establish a regional RPPLH, they were faced with nothing less than perplexity. The agency invited a team of academics to consult on ways to move forward with the planning. Data was collected, and scenarios were modelled. A working group was established, consisting of different agencies that were responsible for particular sets of data and sectoral issues. Conflicts, of course, were unavoidable. The Agricultural Agency, for instance, urged for the protection of the said permanent agricultural regions due to the fact that population growth in West Java has been quite exponential while arable lands have been declining rapidly. The Settlement Agency begged to differ. Urbanisation in West Java has been occurring at an accelerated rate as industrial developments have attracted more people to the cities and the surrounding areas. The Irrigation and Water Resource Agency claimed that although water supply in general is sufficient to cater for domestic, agricultural, and industrial needs, its distribution is uneven. This means that catchment areas need to be protected to ensure that the supply of water can be regulated, while at the same time, infrastructures such as dams should also be built in strategic areas to evenly distribute this flow of water across the province.

Facing this situation, the actors again returned to data, in a process of simplification of the assemblage through "rendering technical" its otherwise unruly nature (Li, 2007). The academic team developed several models to predict environmental conditions in the province over the next 30 years. On the basis of population growth and distribution, the models predicted the carrying capacity of each region in terms of food, water, waste, and pollution. This resulted in a set of priorities of the environmental plans and agenda for the specific regions, depending on the type of ecosystem services provided and the potential environmental pressures in those regions. So, for instance, because the ecosystems on the northern coast of Java have a strong potential as food providers that outweighs pressure from projected population growth, the region's strategic environmental priority is to "reduce the environmental pressure of food producing ecosystems" by "conserving and protecting the productive agricultural areas in the region" and "controlling the rate of land conversion from agriculture to non-agriculture" (Dinas Lingkungan Hidup Provinsi Jawa Barat, 2019: 179). In West Java's provincial RPPLH document, this priority is set specifically for 14 (out of 25) regencies/municipalities, which contain the specific food-producing ecosystems, particularly on the northern coast of West Java. What this then means is that for these regencies, the priority to protect their agricultural areas should also be explicitly stated in their regency-level RPPLHD.

However, the planning and development priorities that were set up in RPPLHD did not align well with other interests. Due to the complex issues involved, deadlocks between agencies, and a lack of clear policy implementation in support of RPPLH, the establishment of RPPLH as a planning tool created a loophole for the state and private sectors to find their way into the development planning process. One official at the provincial level, for example, lamented the fact that the Jakarta–Bandung high-speed railway and the hydroelectric dam projects still proceeded even with the existence of RPPLH and other environmental instruments. On the one hand, she observed the potential of RPPLH, if and when established and taking effect, to change how environmental governance worked (which would strongly benefit the environment). This then pushed the task force to accelerate their process, in the hope that the sooner the RPPLH was completed, the less damage development projects would cause to West Java's landscapes. However, on the other hand, she was also sceptical whether it would indeed have such an effect, considering that development projects were often strongly backed by officials at the national level and big businesses. This scepticism would prove to be correct as years later, Indonesia's President Joko Widodo pushed a new law that would enable national strategic projects to go above and beyond the existing planning. This will be further examined in Chapter 5.

The unintended effect of a productive failure

At this stage, if taking a traditional view of governance, RPPLH can perhaps be seen as a failed project on so many levels. At the conceptual level, the idea of replacing the existing environmental planning schemes with RPPLH is a little too stretched. RPPLH requires an almost entirely new way of planning, with social and ecological data being used as the basis for regional and spatial plans. However, these data ranges have not been fully agreed upon, with academics analysing and interpreting them in different ways. Every method of analysis would result in a different basis for planning. For example, one geographer suggested that the analysis be made using a spatial grid $(0.9 \times 0.9 \text{ km}^2)$ as the smallest unit (RPPLHD Jawa Barat, 2019). This grid contained layers of spatial data, from soil characteristics, population, and forest coverage to infrastructure. An ecologist, on the other hand, would focus on an ecological region (eco-region) as the unit of analysis, in which all development plans would be adjusted to the ecological characteristics stretched and the ecosystem services provided. The two approaches conflicted with each other because the resolutions at which the data were taken resulted in different ways of understanding the ecological phenomena in hand and, consequently, the planning strategies formulated.

From an organisational point of view, RPPLH necessitates intensive coordination not only between sectors (agriculture, forestry, environment, mining, etc.) but also across hierarchical levels (central, provincial, and regional). During the Soeharto regime (prior to 1998), this complex coordination might have been possible, thanks to strong top-down control from the central government. However, after the fall of Soeharto, the discrepancies between Java and the outer islands as well as the regional dynamics triggered a push towards decentralisation (Talitha et al., 2020), where provincial and regional governments have a range of rights and the authority to govern their own territories. This includes, among others, public health, housing, agriculture and food security, environment, as well as development and spatial planning (Law Number 23 of 2014 on Regional Autonomy, Article 12). In this regard, the central government would only provide advice, assistance, and monitoring to ensure that regional development is beneficial to the wellbeing of the population. This brings a certain dilemma to the implementation of RPPLH, partly because while certain aspects of environmental governance stay within the authority of the central government, the way these aspects inform regional development planning is in the hands of the provincial and regional governments. In its current state, the coordination process undergone in order to formulate RPPLH seems too messy and complex to be successful, let alone implement it to safeguard and monitor national and regional development programmes.

What looks to be a failed governance scheme, however, has led to something unintended and, one may argue, productive. This production, intended or not, is actually what defines the assemblage (Buchanan, 2021: 47). The messy entanglement of actors in this peculiar process of planning and managing the environment brings forth novel ways of coordinating and making sense of data. Government agencies anticipate the use of a broader spectrum of data for their decision support system. Negotiation and compromise processes, rather than a top-down hierarchical coordination, begin to take shape. At the same time, the failed project also opens up ways for the public to know more about RPPLH, the way it works, and how monitoring and planning can be further democratised. Universities and research centres hold training courses for professionals wanting to acquire new knowledge and skills related to RPPLH. Although RPPLH as a whole does not work, parts of it (particularly the environmental-assessment bits) remain one of the prominent tools to use in various environmental compliance measures. For example, the initial part of formulating RPPLH is to determine the carrying capacity (the extent to which natural resources can support human activities) and load capacity (the extent to which the environment can withstand pollution and burdens), which is currently a well-known concept that is often used in companies' environmental impact assessment (EIA) and the government's strategic environmental assessment (SEA). The latter is a transitional instrument for environmental assessment (supposed to be integrated with RPPLH) which is now used as a prerequisite for spatial and development planning.

Notwithstanding the fact that strategic national projects such as a high-speed railway, nickel mining for electric vehicles, and hydro-electric dams can still proceed without any environmental planning, public scrutiny is now at play, and with new ammunition to support their cause for that matter. In the province of West Papua, environmental NGOs pushed the provincial government to declare theirs as a Green Province, accompanied by a collaboratively crafted RPPLH document that functions not necessarily as a planning document *per se*, but as a strong statement made towards the central government to stop massive economic development in the region and instead shift to green economy in the form of carbon trade, habitat offsetting, and ecotourism. Public consultation, which is a necessary stage in the formulation of RPPLH, is also a venue that opens dialogues between community groups, NGOs, the private sector, and the government in regard to environmental planning. For NGOs and community groups alike, the event is particularly important in channelling their concerns about their local environmental issues, which need to be integrated into the planning document. Thus, although RPPLH is a work of multiple actors within the bureaucracy, when brought to the wider public, it pushes other actors to rethink how environmental management and protection are supposed to be done.

The multiplicity of intended and unintended processes

Unintended but desirable outcomes of IP-Suisse

In the case of IP-Suisse, we observe how the unpredictability of an assemblage resulted in not one but a multiplicity of consequences and novel trajectories. When IP-Suisse entered the Swiss AEG assemblage, it initiated and stimulated several processes (Forney, 2021) which led to a diversity of outcomes, some of which were perfectly aligned with the objectives of the participating organisations, others were unintended but acceptable to the actors, while others still were unwanted and unanticipated. The point here is not so much to decide what was (or was not) planned, intended, and anticipated, as it is to highlight the diversity of what emerges from an assemblage and the uselessness of assessing governance only through the lens of achievements.

Since its inception over two decades ago, IP-Suisse has grown to become a key player in the Swiss agricultural sector. More than 18,000 farm businesses are members of the organisation, which represents about 20% of all Swiss farms. Among them, around 10,000 are certified with the IP-Suisse label. In several key industries, the IP-Suisse standard covers a large part of the production, including wheat where around 40% of the market carries the ladybird label. Farmer members seem to engage enthusiastically in the promotion of biodiversity on their farms, totalling far more points (40% more on average, according to the IP-Suisse website[1]) than what is required by the standardised point system (see Chapter 2 for a more detailed explanation of this system).

All these indicators are producing a narrative of unquestionable success. But is it really the right way to think of the outcomes of the label's development? Does this interpretation give a true account of the complex processes that are going on in the Swiss AEG assemblage? If we engage seriously with the everyday experiences of the actors involved in the assemblage, we soon discover that there is never just one, but many stories to be told, which reflect the multiple faces of everyday AEG. These many stories do not necessarily align with one another. They are expressions of coexisting processes and tensions that animate the Swiss AEG assemblage and in which IP-Suisse, as an organisation, a food label, and a certification scheme, plays diverse roles. More particularly, looking at the everyday governance points to stories that remain untold because they touch upon outcomes that were unanticipated and unwanted. Often those effects of governance practices remain overlooked as they are not reflected in the usual indicators mobilised for assessing the success of policies and strategies.

Alongside and beyond the success story of the rapid growth of IP-Suisse (as based on quantitative indicators such as number of members or biodiversity points cumulated), other processes have deployed around IP-Suisse and the related web of relations. The assemblage reveals its capacities to serve an experimentation field. Actors engage with others, adjust their practices, and explore new ways of interacting, all this creating the dynamics of the assemblage and producing processes that go well beyond the explicit objectives of the governance practice.

For individual farmers, or at least some of them, IP-Suisse certainly offers a place to build new involvements and dynamics around more environmentally friendly practices. One farmer explained how, for him and his brother, joining IP-Suisse was part of a process of learning to farm differently. He learned not only about some of the sustainable methods used in farming and pest management but also about the care for the crops, which led him to observe, learn, and know about nature in a way that differed from what his father had known before.

This story also tells us that labels and organisations are not the alpha and omega of farmers' learning processes. Farmers might be encouraged by premium prices or stimulated by an existing community of practice, but they do not stop at standards. Often, they do more and differently. IP-Suisse appears here to be a milestone in a longer journey and arguably an easier step that allows for a progressive onward move. This desire to learn and experiment is not limited to farm practices. As an example, another farmer member built on the IP-Suisse network to develop Swiss production of quinoa. The process was largely facilitated by the use of the levers offered by the organisation to convince retailers, find mills and collecting centres and other producers, and finally set up a new value chain. As it happens, IP-Suisse farmers are often presented as dynamic and proactive, displaying some kind of pioneering spirit. This is reflected in the image of the organisation as reactive and open to experimentations.

A dense network, direct access to farmers, readiness to try, and flexibility are qualities that IP-Suisse's partners value greatly. However, beyond short-term market ventures, IP-Suisse also plays a more central and structural role in collective experimentation and knowledge creation. As a representative of a large industrial baker presented it, "IP-Suisse is our agricultural department, so to speak". He illustrated this by mentioning the example of trying to launch Durum wheat production in Switzerland, which had never been done before. As the baker put it, all are not "pure success stories". However, the various connections developing around the IP-Suisse organisation and actors of the assemblage—farmers, processors, retailers, etc.—create an environment that facilitates collective experimentations, notably around the development of new productions and value chains.

Another example shows how this experimentation space developing around IP-Suisse has some potential for stimulating a deeper transformation of the food system. As the use of pesticides in Swiss agriculture was being intensely debated in the run-up to a popular vote on a potential ban (Finger, 2021), with most of the farmers' organisations being against this ban, IP-Suisse was contacted by a middle-size industrial baker who wanted pesticide-free wheat for its flour. IP-Suisse took up the challenge and launched a call among its members. In less than 30 hours, the organisation could secure quotes for the required 3,000 tonnes of pesticide-free grain.

As we can see here, the IP-Suisse assemblage does produce many different processes of learning: about collaborating between partners, how to farm differently, how to grow new kinds of crops, how to build value chains based on ideas of sustainability, etc. Through the many collaborations and joint experimentations, actors engage together in a cumulative process of learning, which includes cross stimulations and synergies, and foster a dialogue around sustainability in food systems, by means of a pragmatic approach.

The unwanted side of IP-Suisse

Looking at governance practices from the perspective of the wider governance assemblage in which they are located allows us to identify and understand better some of their unexpected results. The governance assemblage produces its own processes and dynamics that traverse the governance practice. These wider processes influence greatly what emerges. As a modern democracy, the Swiss state builds on a massive bureaucratic apparatus. As we have seen, agriculture is an important political sector which redistributes huge amounts of money through a complex system of payments to farmers associated with environmental standards as well as specific schemes. Such policies are organised around bureaucratic instruments of accountability that are deployed to register and control farmers' claims for state money.

In the IP-Suisse assemblage, those instruments are very influential. As already said, there is strong concordance between policy standards and some IP-Suisse standards. The direct payments (and the biodiversity point system) are designed in a way that gives farmers little room for manoeuvre, leaving only the choice between a selection of practices related to payments or points. The system is not made for testing, experimenting, and learning. As bluntly put by a civil servant from the Federal Office for Agriculture (FOAG), when asked about the role of farmers in the agri-environmental policy, farmers are simply expected to implement what has been set by the standards.

However, "to implement" means not only to do agriculture differently. In order to participate in state-policy programmes or certification schemes, farmers primarily have to fill out a long list of forms and registers. Before mastering the agronomic challenges of agri-environmental practices, they have to understand the administrative system set up by those programmes; to invest time in paperwork; and to strictly record their practices in registers and forms. Farmers' organisations have repeatedly denounced the overload of work caused by administrative tasks. The bureaucratic instruments of governance that are used seem to not only encourage farmers to implement more sustainable practices but also—and mostly—help turn good farmers into good bureaucrats.

From a farmer's point of view, the problem lies not in the volume of work but its nature. Paperwork is generally despised by farmers as not being real work, at least not farmers' work. Many farmers struggle to carry out these tasks that have become central to the economic balance of their farms. A significant proportion of farm revenues depends on them, first of all through the direct payment system but also if they want to benefit from premium prices related to a certification. An IP-Suisse farmer, who seemed to navigate this administrative maze comfortably, still expressed his worries for some of his colleagues who had to face this dramatic increase in administrative and desktop work.

Administrative skills, such as general computing skills, but also the ability and discipline to scrupulously record specific actions, to decipher the AEG jargon, to identify the synergies between different schemes, and develop strategies that optimise gains in relation to the implementation of a given farming practice, become essential for being a successful farmer in this AEG assemblage. In addition, rules and criteria are regularly evolving in all the schemes, and farmers have to keep themselves updated and adapt. A comparative study on psychosocial risks in agriculture, including Switzerland, identifies this continuous change in rules as a factor of insecurity and anxiety for farmers who are under constant fear of failing (Droz et al., 2014).

Pressures on farmers are of course related to the checks that are central to building trust and accountability in the system. And, indeed, every year farmers are financially sanctioned for not complying with the rules. For instance, in a statement to the media, the FOAG said that, in 2016, 16% of Swiss farms had been sanctioned by the state with deductions from their direct payments, which amounted to a total of CHF 8.4 million. Interestingly, however, real misbehaviour seemed to be the exception, with most of those sanctions being given for "unimportant things, for instance forgetting to fill in a form". This statement was confirmed in an interview with the private certifier. In other words, farmers and other actors in the food chain get sanctioned mostly for failures in the accountability system related to misreporting and declarations in the official forms and documents, and not so much for failing to observe the actual environmental requirements. In the practice of checks, this focus on the bureaucratic foundation of accountability systems is reflected in the fact that inspectors will first of all check the multiple documents and forms sitting in the farmer's office or kitchen, and spend very little time and effort to look at the farm, the field, as the concrete results of the farmer's work.

Those who ride the unpredictability of governance practices

Materiality and socio-technical devices

In the case of DS, we want to unravel the many facets of heterogeneity as well as turn our attention anew to materiality and non-human actors. We look at how everyday governance provides insight into the non-linear, open, and fluid nature of assemblages (see also, e.g. Briassoulis, 2019). The key points here are the role of documents (non-human agency) in shaping the agendas and mobilising soybeans as part of an emerging protein transition for Europe; the role of events in circulating the documents (and knowledge) beyond the boundaries of specific scientific expertise; and the unexpected effects shaped by the assemblage at the level of policy-making experts in aligning the aims and actions of DS with the policy community.

We refer to Suchman (2012), who argues that a plan reveals relations between ordering devices and the contingent labour through which it is produced and made reflexively accountable to ongoing activity. She further stresses that such an approach goes against naturalising plans as representations existing prior to, and determining, action. Henceforth, we use documents as devices that constitute multiple actions and which participate in the creation of the architectural design for soy in Europe. Attention to documents and their circulation in different spheres of action points us to a new archaeology of knowledge that not only rewrites the goals and trajectories of action but also redefines the role of soy in the governance assemblage as well as the place of socio-technical devices, such as standards, in the organisation's agendas of change.

To start with, we look into how the scientific research project "Legume Futures" was supported by the European Union as a way of proofing against unintended consequences should an expansion of soya cultivation in Europe be pursued. This positioning of intention was welcomed by the project leader who underlined that if such research had been carried out 50 years ago, many of the environmental costs could have been avoided. In other words, the story is about how actors deal with the unpredictability of governance outcomes, both by trying to limit unintended consequences and, at the same time, by taking things as they come.

DS unearthed many of the socio-material properties of soya as the organisation designed a standard (known as the Donau Soja standard) to be used as a main instrument of intervening in Europe's soya market and of effecting changes in its agricultural practices. These include, for instance, the recognition of soya beans as legumes and the wider family of crops used as important sources of protein in farming systems, as well as their significance in crop rotation in those same systems. These characteristics came to be integrated into a knowledge coproduction process nourished by the diverse human actors involved in the science, business, and political decision-making around this crop. The documents, events, and actions that kept this knowledge process unfolding and evolving came to shape the trajectories the DS organisation was to take. It shaped agendas, planning, and results.

These informed the internal workings of the assemblage and the interactions between socio-technical, spatial, and political dimensions laid out by the DS project. Within a few years, DS established itself as an important player in the soya market in Europe. Not only was the design of the standard and the gradual uptake of the certification and label by numerous actors an indicator thereof, DS also demonstrated its contribution to the doubling of soya cultivation in the European Union, and to a further significant increase in quantities within five years through flows of soya from European countries outside of the European Union. Graphics presented at every DS assembly and conference and in research outputs testified to this, without obscuring the long road lying ahead for covering half of Europe's soya needs by 2025 as planned by DS. The latter conjures up a whole set of other changes that go beyond the techno-economic spheres required in the wider soya assemblage in order for a deeper transformation to take place.

A leading document was produced to delineate soya's role and significance for the wider political and agricultural landscape of Europe. The DS vision drew upon the so-called Theory of Change in economics to design a sustainable soya architecture for Europe with a long-term vision in mind. This is "The European Protein Transition",[2] which was finalised in 2018. It lays down five core lines of action which need pursuing in order to address the Protein Challenge and are required for a European Protein Transition to take hold:

1 Sustainable and responsible imports—whereby the global dimension of the Protein Challenge is signalled.
2 Increased production of grain legumes in Europe—underlined here are not just benefits to ecosystems but also far-reaching benefits to other crops used in rotation, as well as spatial changes in the flows of soya from Eastern to Western Europe.
3 Improved use of existing and new protein sources—this underscores the role of plants as the most important primary sources of protein.
4 Increased efficiency of protein use—feed management being the target here.
5 Healthier diets—this last pillar directs attention to the disconnect between official meat-consumption recommendations and the actual overconsumption of meat.

What DS did was to come up with a "summary of the future", as one of the main contributors to DS ingeniously put it. In this sense, once the long-term visions were set, the architecture itself came to be built "backwards" by searching for the preconditions that would be necessary for the achievement of long-term goals. For the short term (1–5 years), the aims are to raise production standards and switch to 100% certification, stimulate alternative value chains, and incentivise more precise protein feeding. For the medium term (1–10 years), what is required is "bottom-up" innovation tailored to local circumstances; more research and systematic translation at European, national, and local levels; and, most importantly, policy measures to drive diversity of cropping and improve on-farm biodiversity. For the long-term (1–20 years), it is the improvement of plant breeding along with public support for it, and the development of new value-chain infrastructures, such as East–West trading within Europe.

This action plan represents the most recent document that crowns a whole series of previous steps, research projects, thinking processes, consultations, market research, networking with hundreds of regional and national actor groups, etc. Between 2012 and 2017, within the short period of five years, a substantial amount of research was compiled under many formats, such as books, articles, research proposals, reports, and public talks. Many revolve around agronomic knowledge regarding the environmental benefits of legumes, but many others speak to the policy community and thus also articulate much broader interrelations that can be drawn from such research.

This work informed the design of the organisation's instruments and practices of governance, shaped its ethos and the narratives of change mobilised by it, and also drove actions for political change at the national and supranational level. These two streams of actions for building the organisation and building scope for wider political change are held in tension by efforts to demonstrate the business opportunities in respect to the growth momentum that soya presents in Europe, which is sustained by hundreds of members and industries as well as by efforts to flag momentum for wide-reaching change in European agriculture. This latter effort requires acknowledgment and participation from members of civil society, farmers, and scientists. Such a tension is further amplified by the following facts: first, a radical solution in the form of banning soya is not an option due to the stark dependency on soya in Europe's animal production, which has seen exponential growth especially over the last 10–20 years; second, readymade models found in global soya networks cannot be replicated in Europe; third, a simple focus on replacing soya with alternative plants would have a limited impact while also placing responsibility extensively on farmers and consumers. Yet, the piecing together of distinctive possibilities coming from research and practice has led to the development of instruments such as standards and certifications that include GMO (genetically modified organisms)-free soya, a ban on using certain herbicides, the enrolment of mid-chain actors, and the development of infrastructures.

The logics of change and unexpected realignments

The theoretical framings that we draw upon inspire our probe into the logics of change transpiring from the co-constitutive knowledge and practices that drive governance in particularly transformative ways, and lead us to think further about the ways in which social sciences conceptualise actual and emergent transformation processes. Geels and colleagues (2015: 7) underline the importance of paying "attention to adoption and adjustments in existing systems and the realignments between multiple new and old elements" in order to understand the ways in which system architectures are reconfigured rather than look in a more linear manner for the single drivers coming from niche innovation.

Two research documents point us to the complementary dynamics in support of a reconfiguration process in the way these seek to build an alignment between the aims and actions of DS and the policy community (which would thus form a "governance arena for radical change"; see, Delemarle & Larédo, 2014). "Legume Futures", a research report finalised in 2014 (Legume Futures, 2014), and "Legume Transitions", a research proposal submitted in 2016, were instrumental in creating visibility at the level of the European Union. Common to both is that they not only provide economic and agronomic data and analyses based on a variety of tools and methods, they also point out some of the limitations of the current policy environment which are not conducive to change. The reports advocate for currently marginal practices in agriculture, propose the seeds of several actions (some of which DS came to embrace), and, last but not least, respond to the topic *du jour* in European agricultural discourses. There are thus multiple intersecting fields of meaning that are used to transform the "treadmill politics" (Overdevest, 2005) of agriculture.

We have presented some of the intersections between a series of documents that draw to the surface two distinctive movements, one which builds the DS ethos and the other which creates spaces and framings for policy advocacy. These two movements are co-constitutive. The research carried out in "Legume Futures" and "Legume Transitions" shaped the formulation of the European Protein Transition programmatic document and the composition of the Donau Soja Declaration,[3] while the latter two shaped some of the processes of translation and framing that went into the former. Some of the effects and indirect outcomes of the two projects we described earlier became visible in 2018. That year proved to be auspicious with respect to two milestone developments: a new EU project called "Legumes Translated"[4] awarded to DS in October 2018, and an event organised by the Digi-Agri Directorate of the EU Commission, namely, the EU

High-level Meeting on Protein Plants organised in November 2018 in Vienna.

Our exploration of logics of change as articulated by the DS organisation has led us to emphasise how interactions between heterogeneous elements unleash new understandings of sustainability, and how these emerge through governance practices that pull away from the expectations that come with the development of socio-technical means via standards and certifications and into the political constellations formed by processes of reconfiguration. The methodological paths we embraced led us to address how a micropolitical analysis of documents as devices allows us to situate emerging properties and capacities of the assemblage, or what we referred to as unexpected and indirect outcomes, in a meso-level cross-cutting inquiry into reconfiguration. The agency of the unexpected is to be found in those spaces where things do not develop as planned (Bentia, 2021: 15). Therefore, we argue for conceptualisations of reconfiguration that are attentive to the agency emerging from the unexpected, and further of reconfiguration as both process and effect.

Concluding remarks: breaking with failure and success

This chapter has discussed ways in which the messiness of assemblages may lead to unintended consequences and unpredictable trajectories which go beyond simple success or failure. For example, we demonstrated how in Indonesia vested interests, lack of coordination, and conflict between regional environmental planning and national strategic projects did not translate into linear, predictable outcomes for RPPLH. It gave rise to distrust, which in the end brought about novel, unanticipated, ways of enacting AEG in Indonesia. What seems to be a failed project, we later argued, paved ways for a more productive governance.

In Switzerland, the joint emergence of a multifunctionality turn in agricultural policies and the blossoming of certification schemes and food labels have deeply converged in a well-structured AEG assemblage, where private and public instruments work in synergy. However, while assessments of the environmental efficiency of this entanglement of certification schemes and public agri-environmental schemes are mixed, the production of a strong bureaucratisation of AEG, also supported by an emerging digitalisation of governance tools, becomes obvious.

DS's plans to tackle a path-dependent system in Europe based on soya bean flows from overseas has led to the creation of a standard- and certification-based agenda aimed to ensure an increase in the cultivation of soya beans in Europe. More regional and European soya bean value chains would not only decrease dependency on other continents but also significantly enhance environmental benefits and agricultural practices, as they encourage rethinking of livestock feed, seed breeding, and crop rotation methods. A turning-point development emerged with the framing of soya beans as part of a more comprehensive protein-plan strategy for Europe.

Looking from an assemblage perspective, we understand that failure is a " 'necessary consequence of incompleteness' and of the inability to establish and sustain complete control of the complex assemblages involved in any such system" (Malpas & Wickham, 1995: 39–40). The use of complexity and assemblage thinking should enable us to break with a dualistic way of thinking of "system" and its "failures", and instead look at chaos and order as interconnected features of any system, in processes of emergence highlighted in theories of complexity and assemblage (Urry, 2005; Buchanan, 2021). Failure, therefore, may open pathways to different spaces and possibilities, which we need to anticipate.

This is what Buchanan (2021: 124–125) refers to when speaking of "wild policy", which is always in the making, filling in the gap left between what the policy proposes and what it actually delivers. DeLanda (2006) notes that this is mostly understood when we look at governance beyond intention and more in terms of desire (which belongs to both human and non-human actors) instead. By better understanding desire, we may unravel the agency and power that lead to the multiplicity of assemblage and the unpredictability of outcome. In the next chapter, we look into this very aspect.

Notes

1 www.ipsuisse.ch/fr/mission-b/, last accessed 09.06.2022.
2 This document presents the programmatic agenda of the DS organisation. It can be found on the website of the organisation: www.donausoja.org/wp-content/uploads/2022/06/DS_Protein-Strategy-for-Europe-26072018.pdf, last accessed 29.09.2023.
3 See   www.donausoja.org/organisation/donau-soja-and-europe-soya-decla rations/, last accessed 29.09.2023.
4 See www.legumestranslated.eu/, last accessed 29.09.2023.

References

Bentia, D. C. (2021). Towards reconfiguration in European agriculture: analysing dynamics of change through the lens of the Donau Soja organization. *Sociologia Ruralis* 61(4): 663–680.

Briassoulis, H. (2019). Governance as multiplicity: the assemblage thinking perspective. *Policy Sciences* 52(3): 419–450.

Buchanan, I. (2021). *Assemblage Theory and Method.* London/ New York: Bloomsbury.

Capra, F. (1996). *The Web of Life: A New Synthesis of Mind and Matter.* London: Flamingo.

de Zwart, F. (2015). Unintended but not unanticipated consequences. *Theory and Society* 44: 283–297.

DeLanda, M. (2006). *A New Philosophy of Society: Assemblage Theory and Social Complexity.* Bloomsbury: London.

Delemarle, A., & Larédo, P. (2014). Governing radical change through the emergence of a governance arrangement. In S. Borrás & J. Edler (Eds.). *The Governance of Socio-Technical Systems* (pp. 159–186). Cheltenham/ Northampton: Edward Elgar Publishing.

Dinas Lingkungan Hidup Provinsi Jawa Barat. (2019). *Rencana Pengelolaan dan Perlindungan Lingkungan Hidup Daerah (RPPLHD) Provinsi Jawa Barat.* Bandung: Pemerintah Provinsi Jawa Barat.

Droz, Y., Miéville-Ott, V., Jacques-Jouvenot, D., & Lafleur, G. (2014). *Malaise en agriculture: Une approche interdisciplinaire des politiques agricoles France-Québec-Suisse.* Paris: Karthala.

Ferguson, J. (1994). *The Anti-politics Machine: Development, Depoliticization, and Bureaucratic Power in Lesotho.* Minneapolis, MN: University of Minnesota Press.

Finger, R. (2021). No pesticide-free Switzerland. *Nature Plants* 7(10): 1324–1325.

Forney, J. (2021). Farmers' empowerment and learning processes in accountability practices: an assemblage perspective. *Journal of Rural Studies* 86: 673–683.

Forney, J., & Dwiartama, A. (2023). The project, the everyday, and reflexivity in sociotechnical agri-food assemblages: proposing a conceptual model of digitalisation. *Agriculture and Human Values* 40(2): 441–454.

Geels, F. W., McMeekin, A., Mylan, J., & Southerton, D. (2015). A critical appraisal of Sustainable Consumption and Production research: the reformist, revolutionary and reconfiguration positions. *Global Environmental Change* 34: 1–12.

Law, J., & Mol, A. (2002). Complexities: an introduction. In J. Law & A. Mol (Eds.). *Complexities: Social Studies of Knowledge Practices* (pp. 1–23). Durham and London: Duke University Press.

Legume Futures. (2014). *Legumes Futures – Legume-supported Cropping Systems for Europe*. General report.

Levin, S. A. (1999). *Fragile Dominion: Complexity and the Commons*. Reading, MA: Perseus Books.

Li, T. M. (2007). Practices of assemblage and community forest management. *Economy and Society* 36(2): 263–293.

Malpas, J., & Wickham, G. (1995). Governance and failure: on the limits of sociology. *The Australian and New Zealand Journal of Sociology* 31(3): 37–50.

Miller, P., & Rose, N. (1990). Governing economic life. *Economy and Society* 19(1): 1–31.

Overdevest, C. (2005). Treadmill politics, information politics, and public policy: toward a political economy of information. *Organization & Environment* 18(1): 72–90.

Scott, J. C. (1998). *Seeing Like a State: How Certain Schemes to Improve the Human Condition have Failed*. New Haven, CT: Yale University Press.

Suchman, L. A. (2012). *Human–Machine Reconfigurations: Plans and Situated Actions*. 2nd edition. New York: Cambridge University Press.

Talitha, T., Firman, T., & Hudalah, D. (2020). Welcoming two decades of decentralization in Indonesia: a regional development perspective. *Territory, Politics, Governance* 8(5): 690–708.

Urry, J. (2005). The complexity turn. *Theory, Culture & Society* 22(5): 1–14.

Voß, J.-P., & Kemp, R. (2006). Sustainability and reflexive governance: introduction. In J.-P. Voß, D. Bauknecht, & R. Kemp (Eds.). *Reflexive Governance for Sustainable Development* (pp. 3–28). Cheltenham, UK/ Northampton, MA: Edward Elgar.

Walker, G., & Shove, E. (2007). Ambivalence, sustainability and the governance of socio-technical transitions. *Journal of Environmental Policy & Planning* 9(3–4): 213–225.

4 Power, agency, and desire
in everyday governance

Introduction: of power, agency, and desire

Power

Governance is intrinsically related to the exercise of power, as it aims to change or steer the action of others. In the context of agri-environmental governance (AEG), many actors exert, on diverse other actors, multiple forms of power that coexist and are articulated in the experience of the everyday. In the previous chapter, we have highlighted the multiplicity of processes resulting from assemblages. This coexistence, within the same assemblage, of diverse processes that do not align brings to the fore the role of power in their articulation and their balancing. Processes are supported or resisted by elements, or groups of elements, of the assemblage. They emerge from a balance of power and are shaped by tacit or explicit negotiations. Acknowledging these multiple processes does not suffice to understand what actually emerges from an assemblage.

An everyday perspective on AEG also needs to engage with a theorisation of power. In a Foucauldian sense, power is relational and dispersed. It is somewhat an effect generated by a collective agency in the form of knowledge, a regime of truth, and institutional values. It governs society so that it behaves in certain ways (Foucault, 1977). A Deleuzian way of understanding power, however, goes a bit further. It sees power as something immanent within an assemblage. Power is not separated from the entity that exerts it, rather it is shaped by the interactions of actors—human and non-human—through their desires and agency (Rolli, 2016). Power, in this sense, comes from the relationality of the assemblage, which is exerted by the actors

DOI: 10.4324/9781003271260-4

and elements of the assemblage through coordinations and tensions in such a way that the assemblage holds together, as stated by Allen:

> Power, as I understand it, is a relational effect of social interaction. It may bridge a gap between here and there, but only through a succession of mediated relations or through the establishment of a simultaneous presence. People are placed by power, but they experience it at first hand through the rhythms and relationships of particular places, not as some pre-packaged force from afar and not as a ubiquitous presence.
>
> (2011: 1–2)

It is therefore interesting to see how power has both shaped the assemblage and is shaped through the assemblage. Approaches and theories influenced by assemblage thinking have underlined power in terms of power of association. Actor–network theory points to the role of centres of calculation (Latour, 1987). Practice theory highlights the power that practices themselves hold by simply coordinating and orchestrating relations (Bourdieu, 1977). In a more general vein, the assemblage approach shifts attention to the non-representational (and more-than-representational) dimensions that constitute the fabric of social life and thus offers the possibility to reconsider the emphasis given to the agency of representations, of individuals, and of scale by other traditions of thought. In this way, it lends weight to spatial, temporal, and affective (lived, embodied, practised) relations that glue the elements of the assemblage together in ways that shape its trajectories.

Agency: individual, distributive, and collective

An assemblage is traversed by multiple streams of power. Elements of the assemblage have to navigate those streams in order to reach their own objective. For Tania Li (2007: 264), "assemblage flags agency" as "the hard work" needed to create and maintain connections despite many tensions. However, assemblage thinking also questions agency at the level of the individual, by highlighting the distributive nature of agency. Acting always depends on others. This statement questions the usual understanding of agency as the individual capacity to act autonomously. In assemblage, power at the individual level becomes the capability not to decide for others but to influence and steer the directions of processes of change. Similarly, agency becomes collective and distributive, highlighting the essential role of inter-dependencies and alliances in the realisation of individual desires. Adding onto Tania Murray Li's phrase, we can say that assemblage flags *distributive* agency.

This engagement with the complexity of agency aims at a fine-grained understanding of how power works in governance. As Li (2007: 264) noted, answers to "how" questions deserve more attention in the study of governance. Such questions—how power is exerted in assemblages, how elements are unevenly impinging on the trajectory of the assemblage, or how interdependencies influence agency—are essential at least from three different perspectives. From a democratic perspective, it should help to design more equitable and democratic governance practices. From an environmental perspective, it should contribute to identifying more ecologically efficient solutions. From a social perspective, it affects the cohesive quality of human relationships, drives mobilisation and engagement, and encourages collective responsible actions.

We should, however, emphasise that the power and distributive agency that are embedded within an assemblage do not mean that the assemblage is, in itself, autonomous and self-regulating. This way of thinking would leave us trapped in depoliticising AEG and strip away any deliberate actions to achieve a more sustainable food system. Buchanan (2021: 120–121) warns us of Bennett's (2010) conception of distributive agency, where he argues that "without any sense of how [elements of an assemblage] are interconnected, ... we are condemned to go on untangling and following threads literally forever without being ever able to decide 'this is it!'" We concur, and instead argue for the contrary: assemblage thinking enables us to envision resistance following a status quo, which Deleuze and Guattari refer to as "lines of flight", being in opposition to "lines of articulation" (see also Dwiartama & Piatti, 2016). In this book, we therefore propose a discussion on power and agency that is more than just individual, collective, or distributive (such as what Bennett argues; see Bennett, 2010), but a complex relationship between the three forms of agency.

Desires

Elements of an assemblage come together with desires and intentionalities. *Desire* is an element of the assemblage which can explain and demonstrate how different practices are "glued" together across scales and sectors in ways that significantly define the specificity of particular assemblages and the courses of actions taken. Deleuze and Guattari (1987: 296) argue that desire is infrastructural and of the order of production. This argument is a strong statement in favour of the agency and power of desire. It brings for our analysis understandings as to the consequential nature of desire for the practice of governance in the way in which it both steers as well as changes actions and activities. Indeed, research underlines its outreach and indicates where desires can be captured and situated. Desire is an overflow that is never fully captured by the turbines of definable interests (Windsor, 2015: 157). Desires collectively shape the future direction of the assemblage. While never separated from the other two dimensions of agency and desire in assemblage (individual and distributive), the collective acquires a certain autonomy in the process of ongoing assembling and reassembling. The collective dimension is formed and enacted through activities and practices that bring different actors, different forms of knowledge and governance goals together with the aim of communicating and sharing the ethos of an organisation.

Desires and agency matter because they shape the processes developing in the assemblage, while being the assemblage itself. Encounters and the partial alignment of desires can result in alliances around processes of change. Multiple agendas can align for a shared purpose, but with potential future divisions. Diverging desires can also work to destabilise the assemblage. Therefore, to be an agent is not something that has to be thought of as individual, but as a capability of influencing the wider assemblage on the basis of interrelations and interdependencies, with allies who can be humans, institutions, machines, skills, or ideas.

Assemblage also entails capacities, which is assemblage that has yet to materialise, but drives actors to do so by condensing and attracting desire. Capacity is an accumulation of desires that mobilise an assemblage towards a particular trajectory—in the case of AEG, towards the sustainability that we aim to achieve. We further reflect this in our cases. In relation to IP-Suisse, for instance, we question how power relations are characterised by a high level of interdependency—both strong dependency on one retailer and counter-power through renewed alliances.

Building power and agency through alliances and interdependencies

The synergies within the IP-Suisse assemblage described in Chapter 2 are not a tale of harmony and egalitarian collaboration for a common good. They are made much more of tensions and conflicts than of shared interests. For instance, farmers, industries, and retailers have diverging interests in terms of price formation for every step in the value chain. Collaborations in the certification scheme are motivated by a diversity of underlying objectives. The sustainability officer of a meat-processing company spoke of expanding its capacity to reach farmers and influence their practices in order to mitigate the environmental impact of its employer. A farmer spoke of his taste for new challenges and will to leave behind what he considered to be bad practices. A representative of IP-Suisse talked about securing added value for the commitment to environmental actions done on farms; the marketing officer of a supermarket chain commented positively on the good balance between sustainability branding and still-accessible prices. The fact that the IP-Suisse assemblage continues to grow successfully does not mean that all these tensions are somehow neutralised, but it makes obvious the role of power within the assemblage. Power relations are obviously essential dynamics that at the same time result from the coming together of the elements of the assemblage, and shape how the elements of the assemblage stick together.

While other approaches tend to clearly identify power relations and dominant positions, the multiplicity of relations that characterise the assemblage complexifies the question of power. The way a dominant position leads to the actual possibility of controlling or shaping the assemblage is not clear. Let us take the example of the decision of the big retailer, who clearly holds power, to impose pesticide-free production for all the wheat flour used for the bread it sells. This decision was made possible only because IP-Suisse already experimented with grain production without any chemical in partnership with another, smaller, industrial baker. Similarly, all the actors involved in seed selection in the past decades made available wheat varieties that are adapted to the Swiss context and quite resistant to many diseases. The state subsidies paid for pesticide use reduction made the new standard more economically viable for farmers, who could feel in public debates and political decisions that they would anyway have to move progressively away from the use of products that are damaging to health and the environment. Also, wheat and its specific property could be included in this programme, while other, more vulnerable crops, such as rapeseed, would not fit. We could continue with this list for many pages, but the point is already clear.

One could say that the retailer decided unilaterally on this ban on pesticides and that the whole IP-Suisse assemblage was forced in one direction by one dominant actor, and it is a fact that not any actor could have such an influence on the assemblage. However, at the same time, ignoring the many efforts made by a multitude of actors is quite unfair. It would actually make us blind to the complexity of acting, and therefore, blind to the distributive nature of agency in assemblages. Indeed, a relational understanding of power recalls the concept of distributive agency that characterises assemblage thinking (see Chapter 2). As you may remember, Bennett (2010) uses the metaphor of the bicycle on a gravel road: the precise trajectory results from the action of many elements. Building on this, elements of a governance assemblage might well have their individual plans, but what results and actually happens depends on the actions of many. From an assemblage perspective, no one can govern alone, not even a very dominant supermarket chain. The most powerful elements of the assemblage still need the others to act and cannot totally control what emerges from this joint action.

The assemblage is defined not by the addition of its elements or by the relations that constitute it, but by what it produces. And what it produces is the result of the accumulation of those multiple agendas and agencies. This means that none of the elements of the assemblage can decide alone what the whole will become. Elements are dependent on others to achieve their goals, and their goals and actions are themselves influenced by those of others. Of course, some actors have a stronger influence within a specific assemblage, but none can control all of its productions. The agency of the assemblage is distributive. As in the image used by Bennett (2010), although someone can hold a bike's handlebars, all the pebbles on the road, the wind, and other road users will still influence its trajectory. Annemarie Mol's deconstruction of the statement "I eat" exemplifies well that actions—which we usually think of as individual—are always made possible by the action of others, humans and non-humans. As she concludes, such a relational engagement with action "suggests a model of doing that does not just elude centralised control but also defies individualism"

(Mol, 2021: 77). This distributive agency of the assemblage results from the complex accumulation of multiple agendas—or, from our perspective, desires—and agencies. "Distributive" in this sense means a set of interactive, consequential, encounters, convergent processes (e.g. deliberative governance), colliding forces (e.g. different goals of governance), or interdependent actions. This is what could be called the "context" of power and that which shapes the collective dimension of the assemblage. This ultimately circumscribes the co-creative and co-constitutive processes which animate the life force of assemblage. In other words, Deleuze and Guattari invite us to understand the organising logics that define assemblages. Concepts such as desire, attractors, and the collective dimension conjure up its dynamics. Acknowledging the agency of numerous elements of the assemblage does not erase or minimise the question of power, it makes it even more complex. Not only power is always relational and depends on the agency of others to be exerted, actors too are entangled in multiple relations of power.

The power exerted by the federal state and its capacity to introduce new agri-environmental policies sparked the idea itself of creating IP-Suisse in the minds of its founding members. The alliance with supermarkets that hold a dominant position in the food systems has been a core axis of the certification strategy. In other words, the assembling of the IP-Suisse certification scheme was built on the combination of two separate streams of power. Of course, there was a price to pay in this alignment with the already most powerful actors, which would expand their capacity to weigh in on and influence the IP-Suisse assemblage. In such a situation, alliances and conflicts are blurred categories and not easy to differentiate. Large retailing groups have concentrated in their hands a good share of the power in current food systems, and this is certainly true in the case of Switzerland. The partnership between the retailer Migros and IP-Suisse started from the very beginning. This means that the whole organisation of the label and certification has been shaped by this partnership. In fact, the Migros group does not only buy 80% of the wheat but also a large share of all the other products certified by IP-Suisse. At the same time, IP-Suisse has been involved at the core of Migros's sustainability strategies for Swiss food products. The farmer organisation is deeply integrated in several value chains supplying Migros supermarkets, with key roles in quality and quantity management. Migros also owns the processing facilities through which those products transit. The retailer is therefore a significant gatekeeper controlling access to the market. Still, the farmer organisation also controls access to farmers and this central role is acknowledged by actors in the food industry. This is suggested by Clapp and Fuchs's (2009) model of corporate power in food systems. In addition to the control over infrastructures and markets, retailers exert considerable power on the narratives and images that accompany products. A good illustration of this discursive power was the use for more than 20 years of Migros's own brand, "Terrasuisse", imposed on IP-Suisse-certified products. Until recently, the retailer refused to use the official brand and logo of IP-Suisse (the ladybird). Interestingly, Migros and IP-Suisse announced jointly in 2020 that they would strengthen their partnership and that this would also include the use of the ladybird on the packaging instead of the label Terrasuisse. In fact, the brand Terrasuisse was never seen as very successful and the increase in the fame of the ladybird, notably thanks to a new partnership with another retailer (i.e. Denner), most likely played an important part in this reversal in Migros's communication strategy and capability to keep control over these important symbols.

The concentration of instrumental, structural, and discursive power in the retailing sector (Clapp & Fuchs, 2009) seems to also be a reality in the IP-Suisse assemblage. This power would not exist without the action and participation of many elements of the assemblage, actors in the value chains, consumers, policies. The certification scheme itself contributes to the centralisation of power over retailers, notably through the implementation of a strict unidirectional traceability paradigm. This traceability is based mostly on the identification of the products and actors, on the collection of samples at every step of the chain, and on the precise documentation of the circulation of goods through the food chain so "we can track down"—in the words of a certifier—products from the package in the supermarket to the farm, across every step of the value chain. The whole process seems to be oriented upstream, focusing the attention on possible failures happening on the way to the shop. Targeted checks—beside the usual random checks conducted under the certification scheme—are generally activated on the initiative of the retailer. The whole assemblage seems to create attention and controls that always look to the production side of the chain, as we later also explain similarly in the case of Donau Soja (DS). The few errors made in the supermarket shops we heard from were tolerated, whereas mistakes by farmers or intermediaries led to financial sanctions. The logic of the certification reflects well the double movement of power in the assemblage, where power relations shape the assemblage at the same time that the assemblage produces power relations. If the power of the retailer results from the concerted actions of many actors, the same can be said for counter-power developing in the assemblage. Alliances are made and new actors are brought in the assemblage reconfiguring power relations, as we have seen, for instance, with the arrival of the hard discounter Denner.

Obviously, state policies exert a major influence on the IP-Suisse assemblage, setting the legal and political frame that defines the governance instruments and their fundamental logic. So do the retailers, who mobilise certification in developing new markets and building their environmental legitimacy. Less directly, the certification agencies, as long-term partners, influence the development of IP-Suisse's standard in dialogue with the farmers' organisation, translating general propositions into schemes and measures that are compatible with the logics of certification. The same goes for all the elements of the assemblage. Simply by existing in the assemblage, and then by trying to follow the course of their desires and finding allies, they collectively build their agency, which is never fully individual.

One question, however, lingers: if power and agency are never fully individual, and if power is exerted through a continuous process of becoming among complex assemblages of actors, then what makes a certain form of power (in this case, one that seems to be dominated by a single actor, i.e. the retailer) stable and not others? In many literatures, power/control is most often unidirectional. It is seen as something exerted from the top down or from the centre towards the periphery. Even when we talk in a Foucauldian sense, the relationality of power implies that the sovereign/disciplinary institutions are those that gain the most benefits from the power relations.

However, we argue that, in an assemblage approach, not only is power relational and multidirectional, it can also be transient. Of course, in strongly territorial assemblages, power relations can be fairly stable, as shown in the case of the IP-Suisse assemblage. However, as power is always in the making, there are cases where power can be manifested differently in response to the changing arrangements and alignments of actors within an assemblage. It can be at once centralised and stable, and yet, through these changes, transformed into an entirely new form. In the case of Indonesia's RPPLH, we look at the ephemerality of power as an encounter within new assemblages (Faier & Rofel, 2014; Huang, 2020).

Encounters of power and ephemeral assemblages

As asserted in Chapters 2 and 3, RPPLH is seen as a device that emerges from the central government's attempt to build legitimacy on environmental governance over the regional and local governments. Whether this instrument works is yet to be ascertained. What seems clear is that the introduction of RPPLH as a component of the environmental governance assemblage created a moment where power dissolved and re-emerged in a novel form. In documenting this distributed power, we once again look at the way in which West Java's Environmental Agency pushed the RPPLH that they led to build it into their provincial development planning.

West Java's Environmental Agency is a small, sometimes insignificant, agency amidst the larger government offices, such as the planning, agriculture, industrial, and public work agencies. Regardless, the officials bear a heavy mandate—they have to ensure that all development projects, economic activities, and government programmes comply with the environmental standards set. The agency has always been under public scrutiny in regard to their responsibility to safeguard the ecological integrity of West Java's landscape amidst development pressures. When the public sees there are floods during the heaviest rains, all eyes are set on the reasons why the Environmental Agency is unable to regulate factories along the Citarum River (the largest river in West Java, which connects major industrial areas and cities in the province). However, business often sneers at the agency for being a hindrance to development—setting too low a pollution threshold and implementing too strict rules that might leave business inoperable.

So, when an opportunity arose to use an instrument potentially as strong as a development plan, the Environmental Agency took a lead in bringing its desire into an assemblage of environmental governance. They coordinated with various other offices to bring their analysis of environmental conditions in West Java onto the table. They consolidated data, reports, and statistics to make a valid planning point. They worked with academics and consultants to gain insights into data interpretation and meanings. Ultimately, they tried to convince the ministry about how their RPPLH had been planned succinctly and on a strong scientifically legitimate basis. RPPLH, here, acts as more than just a document or scheme. It is something that reconfigures actors in a new set of assemblages.

What we then witnessed within West Java's Environmental Agency is how an institutional actor (and the human actors within) has made use of this new assemblage to exert a form of power that is different from what is usually exerted by the central government. The centrality of planning now shifts to the Environmental Agency. However, whereas the central government exerts its power through regulations, instructions, and top-down commands all the way to the regional level, the current power is instead moving sideways, making use of negotiation and coordination. The Environmental Agency negotiated with other agencies through data, and coordinated through the creation of a document. Let us take a few examples to illustrate.

It is clear that the Environmental Agency has a certain desire to delimit the extent of economic development in the province through strict environmental regulations and standards. It aims to prioritise environmental logic over others. RPPLH allows the agency to do so by demonstrating how environmental data (water and air pollution, human population, rate of deforestation, or soil degradation), if configured correctly, is apparently connected (in a statistical sense, correlated/influenced by) to other sets of data for which other agencies are responsible (e.g. water availability, irrigation infrastructure, settlements, agricultural productivity). The agency might show, for instance, that the settlements encroaching on the hinterland reduce the availability of clean water and, in effect, increase the health risks to the population. In response to this, the agency argued that the Settlement Agency needed to shift the focus of its programme to a different area or limit the development altogether. The same holds true for the way the Manufacturing Agency should change where and how industries are operated. Through data (as translated through the RPPLH assemblage), the Environmental Agency de- and reterritorialises the provincial landscape by allowing and closing other actors' access to one or other territory.

The Environmental Agency also coordinated through the creation of a document. As the lead actor in the formulation of RPPLH, the agency makes recommendations on how coordination between agencies is supposed to be conducted to achieve the province's environmental goals. For every region that is assigned a certain environmental and developmental objective (e.g. the north coast of West

Java being assigned the role of a sustainable agricultural region), the agency appoints the Agricultural Agency to take on the main responsibility of ensuring that environmental standards are being integrated into the food security objective. Similarly, at the central regional level, the responsibility is assigned to the Plantation Agency, and in the metropolitan area, to Settlement and Transportation Agencies. These agencies are required to coordinate with the Environmental Agency in each aspect of development, ensuring that environmental impacts are taken into account. For the Environmental Agency, therefore, RPPLH is seen to build a coherence between sectors at the same regional level, under its coordination.

The ministry, however, looks at this effort rather differently. From their perspective, RPPLH is a way to build coherence between national and regional planning. The RPPLH document at the national level should be the main reference for the lower-level RPPLHD. It is like looking at a higher-resolution map, where the detailed plans are actually derived from the bigger picture. It is another desire that leads such power to be exerted on the other actors within the assemblage. The central government, it seems, looks at power as part of a plain vertical relation, whereas the Environmental Agency would argue that power manifests through their assemblage, where governance may go top down, bottom up, sideways, or across. While the Environmental Agency acts as the centre of calculation in the context of RPPLH, its centrality is more rhizomatic rather than geographical in nature.

We therefore understand that a new power is exerted from the encounter between the assemblage of vertical hierarchies, which is a complex arrangement held together through rules and regulations that enable the ministry to issue commands to the regional governments, and the assemblage of horizontal arrangements brought about through coordination and negotiations between regional offices and agencies. We refer to the work of Faier and Rofel on what they termed the ethnography of encounters, as well as DeLanda's transient assemblages. Their study focuses on how culture is "made and remade in everyday life" (Faier and Rofel, 2014: 364) not within a single population, but through encounters between two or more cultural groups. Huang (2020) extends the analysis to investigate the establishment of an energy initiative that emerges not from a well-planned project but a messy series of events. We think that the argument can also be applied to the notion of transient power, as shown in the case of RPPLH.

One thing to underline in the case of environmental governance in Indonesia is that it never truly manifests in a stable set of
assemblages (see Chapter 2 for an elaborate narrative of the history
of environmental governance; or see Dwiartama, 2018). These continuous changes substantiate the idea that what appears to be stable is
instead a "quasi-stable state" (Dwiartama & Piatti, 2016), subject to
both weakening and reinforcing forces, or in Deleuzian terms, lines of
flight and lines of articulation. However, what is interesting about this
particular case is that RPPLH, in both its machinic (a document) and
enunciative (an idea or scheme) senses, acts somewhat as a disruption
that enables us to see this encounter between two sets of assemblages
in their processes of de- and reterritorialisation. In a Latourian sense,
this is analogous to unravelling a black box (Latour, 2005), or to
foregrounding the infrastructure of an assemblage (Star, 1999).

Our concern, however, is not only to see how assemblage is shaped
but also, therefore, how power is exerted as a relational effect of the
said encounter. RPPLH, in this case, enables a reconfiguration of
actors and manifestations of different power relations. It has shifted
one actor to the foreground (the Environmental Agency) and the
others to the background (the Ministry of Forestry and Environment,
the Regional Planning Agency), while introducing new materials (a
formal RPPLH document) and reducing the importance of others (an
AMDAL document). It enables actors to build new connections with
others through coordination and negotiation, such as is the case with
how the Environmental Agency becomes a centre with which other
less powerful actors form an alliance. Tensions are also apparent in the
way the ministry attempts to weaken this alliance through its claims
about what an RPPLH document should be (while the agency argues
that theirs aligns with what the province needs in terms of environmental planning).

The two cases tell us that it takes a lot of effort to maintain an
assemblage, but it would also take similar effort to build or introduce
a new assemblage. Power is indeed an effect of an assemblage, but
through the relationality of power, assemblage is also held together
and broken apart. Power manifests in a spectrum of possibilities over
many directionalities, and is driven through the many desires each of
the heterogeneous actors in the assemblage brings along. Thus, power
is something that is recursively performed. This happens through
acts of controlling the production chains by means of a bundle of
instruments, institutions, and groups of (human) actors; it also happens

through forms of calculation and metrics that are used to reinforce and legitimise actions; and through practices such as meetings that consolidate membership, conjoin inter-professional groups, as well as members of civil society and political representatives, *and* where diverse instruments find new spaces and territories of enactment, as we will show in the case of DS. This is, we think, where desires play a critical role in unravelling how such enactments are actualised.

When agency rules: collective enactments of desire and transnational spaces

Deleuze and Guattari's work builds up in such a way that the generative power of assemblages comes through again and again. Not only does it emerge from the ongoing tensions that territorialise and deterritorialise assemblages, but also at the dynamic interface between the actual and the not-yet-actualised. The tool that Deleuze and Guattari give us in order to get a grasp of how this interface is formed is that of desire. We argue that this interface invites further engagement with the messy and transient/ephemeral nature of assemblages and challenges us counterintuitively to search for the structuring power mechanisms therein. Desires have a significant role in how they operate in the collective dimension of assemblages.

The collective dimension is helpful in bringing a further order of understanding as to the place of motivation, imagination, enthusiasm, affect, beliefs, expectations, and attachments in the workings of the assemblage, and provides scope for analysing how these are reordered through certain practices. A significant role that DS engages with is communicating their understanding of the value of soya for Europe. This is not a clear-cut or straightforward task, but a transactional and situated exercise. This is a form of expertise that DS members take on, embody, and practise consistently. And it is the driver of their craft, the desire that mobilises their work and goals.

The heterogeneity of the assemblage as actualised in the DS organisation includes diverse and different perspectives on the value and promise of soya beans for Europe. What can soya do for Europe, what can it do for farmers, what can it do for the retailers, etc.? Given that the monoculture model of farming became so lucrative in the Americas, how can European soya provide interesting alternatives for industries, processors, and farmers? Could it disrupt existing patterns, could it provide innovative paths for more sustainable agri-food systems?

Organisations such as the World Wildlife Fund or Via Campesina-EcoRuralis, who support the idea of small farmers joining DS, are motivated by the fact that growing soya beans in Europe is a significant measure whereby dependency on the monocrop production based on genetically modified (GM) soya beans can be reduced. This then raises for the said NGOs the question of how farmers are included in the organisation, how they can support DS work, and, in turn, what the benefits for farmers are. Thus, when DS organised the biannual international conference in 2018 in Schwäbisch Hall in close collaboration with a member farming association, some members criticised the fact that out of the nearly 300 participants, very few were farmers, and this undermined their expectations that farmers would be the bedrock of the DS organisation.

For the executive board of DS, however, farmers' presence and power is a question relative to the functions and facilitations opened up by the method of certification and the stipulations of the standard, and also where large-scale soya farming is seen as having a potentially significant impact by disrupting the still dominant monoculture styles of agriculture in Europe, which are blind to better crop rotation, less intensive uses of herbicides, and complexities of the nitrogen cycle. It is in this larger-scale method of farming that soya beans become interesting in the conventional sector. Alternative systems such as the organic model had been adopting soya in crop rotation all along (the certification is taken up by the processors and not the farmers; farmers voluntarily adopt best practices, and regular checks take place). There are complementing tools to the certification process that aim to better assist farmers and the integration of products in value chains. DS focuses on setting training programmes in place as a way to create alliances between actors in the value chain and farmers, and on designing innovative tools—such as the "Protein Partnership"—which are intended as a low-cost alternative to the overseas credit system. For DS executives, farmers are one group of actors alongside equally important groups such as businesses, industries, retailers, and processors who adopt the certification and label and thus increase the presence of DS in the conventional markets.

The two stances in respect to internal reflexivity vis-à-vis the problematisation and pragmatics of the role of farmers in the organisation articulate desire in two different ways: in terms of expectations of a bottom-up change and in terms of an effort to make the standard work by pursuing the nitty-gritty steps of enrolling actors, coordinating actions, and ensuring quality. These articulations of expectations and motivations are part of expressions of desire that unfold along the individual and distributive dimensions of the assemblage. They are strongly attached to the socio-technical as well as institutional expertise of developing the tools and conditions for soya to be cultivated and used in Europe. One consequence of this is that expectations of bottom-up change are in fact transformed through the distinctive design of the certification process which actually relieves some of the pressures and expectations placed on farmers as drivers of change.

Everyday governance is entangled with high economic and political stakes. Powerful actors in the business of soya are invited to consider new opportunities in Europe, and important decision-makers are presented with facts and figures as to the benefits of soya. The economic and ecological values of soya enter competitively multiple spaces of debate, persuasion, and calculation. In this way, plans to develop soya agriculture in Europe involve building diplomatic relations with national and regional state actors (including prime ministers, agricultural, environmental, and trade ministers) within soya-cultivating regions such as Hungary, Romania, Moldova, Germany, and Austria. They play important roles in building alliances, creating new projects and plans, and nourishing the transnational dimension of the vision for soya. The desires that flow into this territory break the boundaries of instrumental rationalities targeting economic and political gains. Several events direct desires into spaces of intense sociality where personal and professional relations can be strengthened, and members and non-members can have lively and open discussions which allow for strengthening personal and professional relations, and for lively and open discussions among members and non-members.

Every two years, DS organises an international conference and opens the stage for the science, politics, and economics of soya to be voiced to a heterogeneous public made up of members and non-members. The different actors of the organisation communicate their results, difficulties, and plans for the future. Every year, smaller events are also organised which also aim to reach out to different publics and inform on the ongoing developments. They also connect powerful allies with influence in the economics of soya across regions. Thus, the Budapest conference honoured Hungary not only as being important in terms of the cultivation of soya beans and adherence to non-GM policy but also its agency as a liaising gatekeeping region between

Western and Eastern European countries which produce soya. This thus confers geopolitical significance on Hungary and the Danube river basin. Such events and meetings lead to the formation of attractors where desires are shaped. In Haug's (2013: 705–708) view, meeting arenas both organise and mobilise purpose and action which have an effect on the meso-level spaces of governance; he underlines the key roles of face-to-face meetings in the interorganisational domain of meso-mobilisation and how these enable coordination across organisational boundaries. All such events outstretch immediate goals and specialised knowledge in that they aim to communicate and translate the bigger picture of the sense and place of soya in terms of the significant contribution it can bring to the wider vision of protein sufficiency in European agriculture, and therefore soya as a driver of a protein transition for Europe (see Bentia, 2021).

Accounts occupy the central stage of meetings. Results-based accounts, administrative and financial accounts, outlook and agenda-setting accounts, environmental, agricultural, social, and political accounts offer the building blocks of evidence that undergird decision-making and planning. Accounts carry desires into the spaces of meetings and enact them in various ways. To a large extent, calculative instruments such as metric evaluations and assessments provide the launching pad of argumentation in favour of leading framings concerning carbon-emission mitigation, the nitrogen cycle, land use, and forest conservation. Most often these point to how soya's systemic features affect the multiple levels of agri-food systems at the same time that these make visible alignments or misalignments with sustainability goals. Accounts do not just articulate the results of the standard and how these meet or do not meet economic and ecological expectations, they also voice propositions for acting on the yet-unrealised potentials of the standard and its value in advancing the protein transition in the European Union. Thus, a high-level EU representative expressed the possibility of developing a protein balance tool to be used as a new sustainable development indicator and as a way to monitor and address the protein-plant deficit in Europe. Such accounts steer desires towards the overarching DS goal, namely, including soya as a tool to rethink the uses of protein in Europe, as well as how it can feature in policy-making. In this way, new trajectories for action emerge which undergird leverage points for sustainability. Such acts of translation not only reposition the importance of metrics in steering change they also redefine the role of soya in food systems. As accounts are staged, many in the audience voice insights into soya being a political issue.

Hence, desire is useful not only in understanding the articulation and negotiation of power relations but also in making visible the relation between articulations of power and sense-making processes that shape the assemblage. Farías (2014) argues that sense-making emerges from the coproduction processes taking place between actual and virtual assemblages. This is a further elaboration of Deleuze and Guatarri's thoughts on capacities which exist in the virtual and have the power to shape actual assemblages. This is where the agencies of soya come into play once again, to show not only how soya is good for business or for the environment but also how soya is good for the transformation of food systems (which will be elaborated in Chapter 5).

As a valuable protein resource, soya can work as a powerful element of the assemblage by contributing to a protein transition in Europe. In this latter capacity, soya becomes the leverage point for reconfiguring agricultural practices, value chains, and international relations, to thus reorient a path-dependent system into new directions. These new directions are embedded in the supraordinate goals of the organisation. These amount to a programmatic plan and vision that advocates and demands new integrated regulatory policies and comprehensive measures to be included in the Common Agricultural Policy Reform. The range of considerations and possible solutions framed in various documents include tackling systemic challenges such as the fact that farming systems are not balanced with respect to the nitrogen cycle, cropping systems are not diverse enough, the excess consumption of animal proteins, etc. The matter of soya beans as leverage points in a protein transition is raised at most meetings and this directs debates beyond the immediate and short-term goals of the organisation and into spaces of possibility for wide-reaching long-term transformation.

Thus, what is being performed is not only a plurality of facts that manifests in documents, metrics, and events but also the heterogeneity of soya's properties and capacities as emerging from their interdependent agencies in wider assemblages. The engine that fires such coproduction of knowledge is the translation of matters-of-fact into matters-of-concern on the one hand, as well as into matters-of-care on the other. This does not mean that the governance practice of DS diverges into random and infinite expressions of desires, or that governance plans represent a holistic exercise of adding up the sum of properties and capacities in one institutional setting.

Meetings contribute to the production of attractors by shaping collective agency. Desires are pulled to gravitate towards attractors that both render DS as an organisation more stable and at the same time influence the wider soya assemblage. Soya is not only made sense of but also redefined in this process. Contrary to the expectations of participants in this event, soya is not the centrepiece of eco-agronomic productivist measures, but rather the blind spot of legislators who are called to actualise its systemic and structural potential for agriculture. In this way, assemblages gain performative power in a number of ways. One of the insights such a perspective brings to the analysis and method of inquiry of assemblages is related to the ontological ordering of governance.

The emergent power of the DS assemblage is strongly related to ways in which the collective dimension is enacted through everyday forms of governance. This means that everyday forms of governance not only participate in shaping the individual and distributive elements of the assemblage by contributing to the actualisation of infrastructures, alliances, and flows of certified soya but also in shaping and changing the very governance practice that realised the formation of the socio-technical arrangement of soya. Thus, the collective dimension of the assemblage has a defining role in enacting the onto-epistemological possibilities embedded in the agencies of soya beans and in the distributed and diverse network of the human actors involved. Furthermore, it is the collective dimension that makes visible the deterritorialising forces of the DS assemblage regarding the wider soya assemblage. At the same time, the collective dimension is, through the enactment of desire, what lends stability and durability to the assemblage.

Concluding remarks: opening to the dynamics of the assemblage

Assemblage thinking "flags agency", to use Tania Murray Li's words. Indeed it does so, but not without implying a redefinition of how agency, along with power, should be understood. The Deleuzian concept of desire is a useful tool in this process, helping us better understand how diverse forms of agency—individual, collective, and distributive—coexist and play in governance assemblages. The convergence of desires empowers individual elements of the assemblage, while the divergence of desires helps destabilise existing arrangements and organisations. From an assemblage perspective no one acts alone. An individual form of agency always participates in a distributive form of agency and what emerges from the assemblage never fully follows individual plans. The interplay of desires defines the direction in which the assemblage will evolve and the processes it will trigger or nurture in wider assemblages. Thus, desire also points to the collective agency and power of a given assemblage to influence the world beyond its own limits. DeLanda (2002) elaborates Deleuze and Guattari's concept of desire by emphasising its infrastructural nature. He introduces the concept of "attractor" in order to define the relation between the actual (i.e. what is) and the virtual (i.e. what could be), and to explain their mutual shaping or, in other words, their interdependence. We have already shown how the virtual helps shape collective desire using the example of DS. While the actual and the virtual are interpreted in research in numerous ways, like for instance as spaces of possibilities or the not-yet-realised outcomes and goals, for us it is important to retain that attractors have an agentic role in influencing the dynamics of the assemblage and, as we develop further in the next chapter, a role in how we define transformation in governance.

References

Allen, J. (2011). Powerful assemblages? *Area* 43(2): 154–157.

Bennett, J. (2010). *Vibrant Matter: A Political Ecology of Things*. Durham and London: Duke University Press.

Bentia, D. (2021). Accountability beyond measurement: the role of meetings in shaping governance instruments and governance outcomes in food systems through the lens of the Danube Soy organization. *Journal of Rural Studies* 88: 50–59.

Bourdieu, P. (1977). *Outline of a Theory of Practice* (translated by R. Nice). Cambridge: Cambridge University Press.

Buchanan, I. (2021). *Assemblage Theory and Method*. London/ New York: Bloomsbury.

Clapp, J., & Fuchs, D. (2009). Agrifood corporations, global governance and sustainability: a framework analysis. In J. Clapp & D. Fuchs (Eds.). *Corporate Power in Global Agrifood Governance* (pp. 1–25). Cambridge, MA/London: The MIT Press.

DeLanda, M. (2002). Deleuze and the use of the genetic algorithm in architecture. *Architectural Design* 71(7): 9–12.

Deleuze, G., & Guatarri, F. (1987). *A Thousand Plateaus: Capitalism and Schizophrenia*. Minneapolis, MN: University of Minnesota Press.

Dwiartama, A. (2018). From 'disciplinary societies' to 'societies of control': an historical narrative of agri-environmental governance in Indonesia. In J. Forney, C. Rosin, & H. Campbell (Eds.). *Agri-environmental Governance as an Assemblage: Multiplicity, Power, and Transformation* (pp. 91–104). London and New York: Routledge.

Dwiartama, A., & Piatti, C. (2016). Assembling local, assembling food security. *Agriculture and Human Values* 33(1): 153–164.

Faier, L., & Rofel, L. (2014). Ethnographies of encounter. *Annual Review of Anthropology* 43: 363–377.

Farías, I. (2014). Virtual attractors, actual assemblages: how Luhmann's theory of communication complements actor-network theory. *European Journal of Social Theory* 17(1): 24–41.

Foucault, M. (1977). *Discipline and Punish: The Birth of the Prison* (translated by Alan Sheridan). New York: Vintage.

Haug, C. (2013). Organizing spaces: meeting arenas as a social movement infrastructure between organization, network, and institution. *Organization Studies* 34(5–6): 705–732.

Huang, J. Q. (2020). Transient assemblages, ephemeral encounters, and the "beautiful story" of a Japanese social enterprise in rural Bangladesh. *Critique of Anthropology* 40(1): 125–145.

Latour, B. (1987). *Science in Action: How to Follow Scientists and Engineers through Society*. Cambridge, MA: Harvard University Press.

Latour, B. (2005). *Reassembling the Social: An Introduction to Actor-Network Theory*. Oxford: Oxford University Press.

Li, T. M. (2007). Practices of assemblage and community forest management. *Economy and Society* 36(2): 263–293.

Mol, A. (2021). *Eating in Theory*. Durnham: Duke University Press.

Rolli, M. (2016). *Gilles Deleuze's Transcendental Empiricism: From Tradition to Difference*. Edinburgh: Edinburgh University Press.

Star, S. L. (1999). The ethnography of infrastructure. *American Behavioral Scientist* 43(3): 377–391.

Windsor, J. (2015). Desire lines: Deleuze and Guattari on molar lines, molecular lines, and lines of flight. *New Zealand Sociology* 30(1): 156–171.

5 Reframing change in governance assemblages

Properties, capacities, and basins of attraction

Introduction: what change is and is not

In 2021, UN Secretary-General António Guterres will convene a Food Systems Summit as part of the Decade of Action to achieve the Sustainable Development Goals (SDGs) by 2030. The Summit will launch bold new actions to deliver progress on all 17 SDGs, each of which relies to some degree on healthier, more sustainable, and equitable food systems. The Summit will awaken the world to the fact that we all must work together to *transform* the way the world produces, consumes, and thinks about food.

(The UN Food Systems Summit, emphasis added)[1]

We must transform our food systems and the relations that constitute them. This imperative has become a globally shared narrative, as reflected in the United Nations Food Summit 2021 communication. Similar calls for a profound transformation are found at diverse geographical and political scales, in diverse institutional contexts, carrying diverse framings of the problems and related solutions. The Milan Urban Food Policy Pact, signed in 2015 by cities worldwide, points to actions at the level of cities and towns aimed at "urban food systems transformation" (Magarini & Porreca, 2019). The World Bank joined the movement in 2020 and created a "dedicated Umbrella Multi-Donor Trust Fund" called "Food Systems 2030". According to its website, "Food Systems 2030 seeks to transform food systems by 2030, fostering healthy people, a healthy planet and healthy economies".[2] We could give endless other examples of this transformation rhetoric being mobilised.

DOI: 10.4324/9781003271260-5

This call for change is not new; scholars have addressed it at many technical levels, and other more theoretical. What is more recent is the apparent unanimity on the need for "transformation". What should be transformed remains, however, ambiguous. Debates on diverse paradigms have animated public and political debates, opposing, for instance, food security to food sovereignty, agroecology to sustainable intensification, as well as technological innovations to a restructuring of power relations between economic actors (e.g. Jansen, 2015; Jarosz, 2014; Scott, 2011). In this chapter, we argue that assemblage thinking can contribute to the debate, first and foremost, by changing the dominant way transformation and change are understood in governance practices.

To begin with, we concur that there have been many ways of understanding change and transformation. The fundamentals of change in society underlie numerous social science theories that discuss change and transformation, including (but not limited to) Marx's metabolic rift (Foster, 1999), Kondratiev's cycle (Barnett, 1998), moments of translation in actor–network theory (Callon, 1986), Holling's adaptive cycle (Gunderson & Holling, 2002), and Geels's transition theory (Geels, 2007, 2010). When social scientists talk about change, they often mean profound and radical changes (Stirling, 2015). In resonance with complexity theory and systems thinking, the assemblage approach develops non-linear attributes entailed in transformation to highlight small but consequential changes for wider-reaching transformations. Small changes, however, are not easily defined and often hidden in the backdrop of several different domains, including socio-technical, socio-ecological, as well as in social norms and values. One approach that addresses how these small changes potentially make a difference is socio-technical transition theory, through the seminal works of Frank Geels (2007, 2010). A socio-technical transition is understood as a process of transition involving not only technological innovation but also the mutual unfolding of societal change interwoven with technology. Geels's multi-level perspective on socio-technical transition seems to advocate for a radical change stemming from a small, niche level that may challenge the existing, stable structures of industry, market, policy, science, and technology regimes. Through a combination of this small change and broader landscape dynamics (exogenous context, e.g., climate change), a regime can be disrupted and readjusted to align with the anticipated state brought by innovations.

Geels's multi-level perspective on socio-technical transition resonates with what is now known as resilience thinking and socio-ecological systems (Folke et al., 2002). A socio-ecological system builds its dynamics within a particular stable state, or stability domain (Walker et al., 2004) and will withstand perturbations and stay within its stable state, unless the perturbation is large enough to change the system's configuration, and shift it into a new state of stability.[3] This stability domain is affected by a combination of different variables: some are large and slow-changing (e.g. a broad political regime or economic system), and others are small and fast-changing (e.g. technological innovations, local movements) (Walker et al., 2006, 2012). This cross-scale relationship is known as panarchy[4] and, to an extent, it resembles Geels's idea of socio-technical transition.

What differentiates these two bodies of literature is the nuances of what they convey as changes. While transition theory emphasises an orderly, controlled, and quite linear change (transition), panarchy opens the possibility of an unpredictable and messy change and the interplay between change and persistence. Stirling (2015), in this case, advances an important argument on contrasting transition with transformation, where the latter aligns more closely with the idea of unpredictable change. A transformation, he argues, involves more diverse and emergent alignments of actors, causes, and values. Drivers of transformation go more broadly than just technological innovations, as they also include what he identifies as emancipatory struggles, which work by challenging the existing structures. On one hand, transformation can be seen as a path towards something profoundly different, in both structure and values. The quote in the beginning of this chapter depicts that sense of values, hopes, and desires attached to transformation. On the other hand, transformation can also manifest as an open-ended process leading to multiple possibilities. In a study on the New Zealand kiwifruit industry, for example, Dwiartama (2017) sees transformation as an effect emanating from an unprecedented moment of crisis and unpredictable future.

From an assemblage thinking perspective, problems are messy, and it is logical to think that answers cannot be simple, and that change will hardly follow a unidirectional line. However, the realisation and implementation of such aims are riddled with numerous obstacles that fuel a linear understanding of change based on modernist and instrumental rationalities. Techno-optimism and a pervasive replacement logic, for instance, do little to bring us closer to a deep awareness that problems are entangled and always complex. This difficulty to move away from a unilinear understanding of change is further reinforced by assumptions of ideals of harmony and equilibrium, equal participation, or the autopoietic functioning associated with some simplistic formulations of holistic system thinking. As a consequence, actors of governance often assume that stability is the norm and that changes, although desirable, are the exception one must advocate for. In reality, however, we often see change happening so rapidly and frequently that an overarching stability is no longer relevant; instead, amidst the ever-changing reality, we must anticipate whatever path a transformation would take us onto, and, as we argue in this chapter, detect less obvious and smaller forms of stability which drive transformation. Governance interventions targeting agriculture and food systems are marked by the same kind of limitations as mobility or energy systems that are, we argue, notably related to a linear and unilateral way of conceptualising change. This, in turn, relates to how we understand governance through an overly dominant logic of control and monitoring. In this chapter, we position ourselves against a linear understanding of change and transformation that is pervasive in most social and political contexts. Assemblage thinking offers an alternative concept of change that points to the limitations of this dominant framing. Importantly, assemblage thinking does not build on the premise of stability, but more on insights resonant with chaos theory and the second law of thermodynamics, where systems exist in ever-changing environments and evolve towards more stable states. Drawing on assemblage thinking, we want to promote conceptualisations of change that are more attuned to the diversity and unpredictability of changes. From our perspective, such a move is of utmost importance in the context of food and agriculture and their governance, the tension between linear simplifications and an extreme complexity of assemblages where all dimensions of life are entangled.

Reassembling change and transformation

To "transform" evokes profound changes at the level of fundamental organising principles of any assemblage. However, assemblage thinking flags change as an ontological dimension of social entities. Assemblage thinking emphasises the changing nature of social life and constructs. What does it mean then to transform assemblages if they are continuously transforming themselves?

Does the differentiation between change and transformation hold in a framing from an assemblage perspective? Those are the fundamental questions related to governance that we want to address in this chapter. From an assemblage perspective, answers first require reiterating a few central ideas around "change", building on the conceptual constructs around multiplicity, unpredictability, desire, and distributive agency.

The first thing we learn from an assemblage perspective on governance is that the main actors of governance practices—institutions and people who design and implement instruments aimed at changing or controlling behaviours, and steering the assemblage—are not external to the assemblage; they are part of the situation they aim to transform. Unfortunately, however, as Arie Rip (2006: 82) noted, "political actors, and more generally, actors with a governance responsibility, will see themselves as somehow outside the system that they have to govern". Acknowledging this participation in the assemblage is, however, the condition for a reflexive governance that could consider that changes in the way of doing governance stand as an essential aspect of achieving transformation.

The *multiplicity* characterising assemblages and their outcomes urges us to anticipate that change never happens alone. Multiple changes happen, and none of them can be fully isolated from the others. In other words, no assemblage is an island. Moreover, their interactions reshape the assemblage, and therefore the reterritorialisation of an assemblage is never entirely predictable. Governance as an action oriented towards implementing or stopping change is, thus, a tricky endeavour. This being said, *unpredictability* does not mean total blindness or an impossibility of anticipation. As Protevi (2006: 21) notes, the "behaviour of chaotic systems" might well be "unpredictable in quantitative detail" but is nevertheless sometimes "predictable in the long run" from a more qualitative perspective. As we will develop later, this speaks for addressing the capacities of assemblages as central elements of assessments.

Multiple changes also imply, quite logically, that we move away from a unilinear perspective of assemblage evolution. There is never a unique path guiding transformation. In governance practices, the consequence is that the changes we want to implement or avoid are always accompanied by other processes of change, unwanted or unintended, which we might well overlook despite their potential effect on the whole assemblage. Therefore, it is necessary to continuously apply a reflexive approach to governance and engage with the multiple changes provoked by governance practices.

We have already highlighted the importance of small changes. While transition theory points to the role of niches in the larger transformations, assemblage thinking alternatively stresses ways in which multiple possibilities are opened up through small changes. Ripple effects in a rhizomatic set of relations might well turn what initially seemed an anecdotal moment into a game-changing series of events. This is notable because small changes can affect and effect relations and *desires* in various ways. Whether big or small, changes are very rarely carried by all the elements of the assemblage. The distributive agencies do not always connect all the dots. This runs counter to the expectations and idealised visions of a uniform change happening simultaneously across the assemblage, for instance, across the realm of consumption and production. This does not mean, for example, that the reordering of value chains does not affect consumers' or producers' attitudes and actions. It rather means that it does so in multiple, partial, and place-based ways: ripple effects and experimentations unfold unevenly.

In the following section, we propose a theorisation of change that acknowledges the multiplicity and unpredictability of assemblages without entirely discarding hope in societies' capacity to anticipate and steer their evolution towards desirable futures, and therefore, without diminishing the power of actors in steering change. If it seems unreasonable to try to control assemblages, their evolution is not random and still follows a certain intentionality, specific operational compositions, and stronger or weaker orderings.

Properties, capacities, and attractors: paths of change

The heterogeneous and unpredictable dimensions of governance practices as assemblages alongside their unevenly distributive agencies (Bennett, 2010) place assemblages in a highly dynamic field of unfolding interactions and processes. Such dynamism does not render assemblages fragile and prone to contingent and fleeting everyday governance outcomes, but, in a more counter-intuitive manner, instead provides the conditions *and* means of change and transformation. In this way, the variety of yearly meetings and conferences connecting both closely and distantly related actors, or the proliferation of the new institutional settings, does not undermine the foundations of the DS organisation; rather, as we show in this chapter, they contribute to enrich the strategies of action and further pull sustainability ends upfront. This resonates with Deleuze and Guattari's view of emergence stemming from the properties and capacities of the assemblages. We start from the two concepts of properties and capacities, which define the current state of the assemblage in its actual organisation and composition and the outcomes (actual or virtual) that emerge from it.

Properties are actualised features of the assemblage and its components at a given time; they are, therefore, limited. Yet they are essential in the making and stabilisation of the assemblage. To give an example, the fact of associating a farmer organisation with a large and powerful retailer is a property of the IP-Suisse assemblage, as is the articulation of environmental data on maps with the provision of development consent in the Indonesia RPPLH assemblage, or the existence of a central office in Vienna dedicated to the coordination of the Donau Soja (DS) assemblage. Properties are, therefore, finite, at least at a given point, as they describe the state of the assemblage. Of course, properties change with time and along the processes of constant territorialisation and deterritorialisation of the assemblage.

Capacities, however, are unlimited as they emerge from infinite possible relations between assemblages and components. In other words, capacities refer to the emergence and the becoming of the assemblage. Capacities can be actual, referring to existing processes that can be documented based on a close observation or analysis, or virtual. Virtual capacities still exist and are real, but different from actual capacities. They refer to what is not yet emerging, but could be, within the space of possibilities of the assemblage. Therefore, they have concrete effects by influencing the action, engagement, and desires of the elements in the assemblage. Coming back to our examples, the association of a large farmer organisation and a major retailer has the actual capacity of introducing significant changes both at the farm level, in agricultural practices related to the IP-Suisse standard, and on the national market, by impacting the prices of agricultural goods and the general availability of more sustainable products for consumers. This can be observed in the short history of the IP-Suisse assemblage. However, the capacity of DS to lead the European Union towards a Protein Policy remains virtual: it guides the action of many and influences the general strategy of the organisation, even if it has not yet been actualised through, for instance, the introduction of a protein policy, or through the formation of a (new) protein assemblage. In other words, the virtual exists in the assemblage through properties, capacities, and desire. To stress once more, capacities in assemblages reach beyond individual agency and beyond human actors, and therefore also beyond, for instance, the managerial notion of capacity-building in the practice of organisations. This emphasis on actual and virtual capacities highlights the emerging nature of assemblages that are defined by what they produce rather than by the sum of their elements. The relation between what is and what could be nurtures these dynamics of change. The multiplicity of the capacities of an assemblage echoes, from a different perspective, the multiplicity of the outcomes of assemblages, as highlighted in the previous chapters.

However, not any change is likely to emerge from an assemblage. The multiplicity of capacities as possible outcomes, actual and virtual, defines a space of possibility in the emergence from the assemblage. These numerous possible evolutions are not chaotic or random. They are limited and bounded by, as well as oriented towards, specific directions that can be referred to as *attractors*. We have already introduced the concept of attractors in the previous chapter and resumed our analysis in this chapter. Dittmer describes attractors through the metaphor of an axis on which the assemblage can evolve:

> Possibility spaces are abstract topological spaces existing in multiple dimensions. Each dimension is an axis on which the assemblage can vary, reflecting the various capacities of its parts or neighboring assemblages. Possibility spaces are structured by how properties of components or assemblages tend to interact. In these spaces, singularities emerge as points that tend to actualize more often. The degree to which the assemblage, as actualized in any given place or time, is near to these attractors indicates how territorialized the assemblage is, and how coherent and stable it appears to us. The ability to vary many of these dimensions and still produce a similar assemblage gives the impression of permanence...
>
> (2014: 393)

The multiple dimensions, or directions, mentioned by Dittmer refer to a set of attractors that influence the trajectory of the assemblage. As attractors are multiple and not always aligned, the aggregated attraction they exert forms what Dittmer calls a "basin of attraction". A basin is not a point of attraction that would provide a clear singular direction of change. The concept of a basin of attraction, as referred to earlier, comes first from the literature on social ecological systems (Walker et al., 2004). However, Dittmer's 2014 proposition introduces a more dynamic understanding of basins, as constituted not of stable points of attraction but rather axes. In this sense, the metaphor of the basin is replete with multiple and possible trajectories—rather than "states"—of the assemblage. Still, these trajectories remain within a space of possibilities where the assemblage's capacities and the attractors' forces of attraction meet. The influence of attractors on the assemblage lies in this conjunction between the internal dimension of the assemblage—its capacities and the desires they provoke— and attractors that generally refer to broader aspirations. A basin of attraction is a visual conceptualisation of directions defining the capacities and possible pathways for the assemblage. It embodies possible futures that already exist through anticipations that shape desires and are prefigured in the actual properties of the assemblage. Desire is then related to the internal perspective on agency and transformation in assemblage, while attractors express the same kind of forces but from an external perspective. To make the difference clearer between resilience and assemblage thinking, we could say that within a resilience framing, which emphasises states of stability, the assemblage/ system is located *within* the basin, while according to an assemblage approach that emphasises the always-becoming nature of things, the assemblage evolves *towards* the basin.

Thinking with Dittmer, we see that changing the basin of attraction can happen through powerful external interventions, like the asteroid that led to the extinction of the dinosaurs, or what we are currently experiencing, which is climate change and biodiversity collapses that will probably lead to dramatic tipping points. These two last examples are interesting because they can be seen at the same time as external and internal factors: most human assemblages are more or less related to the causes of climate change and biodiversity loss, even if, in their everyday experiences, assemblages are mostly confronted to the effects of climate change as an external pressure. In this sense attractors are never totally external to assemblages.

Attractors can take many shapes and forms. Attractors associate enunciative and material elements, just as assemblages do. Ideas and objects gravitate around attractors, building a thread of attraction, stimulating desire within the assemblage. At the same time, attractors form with the aggregation of desires that become strong enough to guide assemblages in a specific direction. The attraction draws a line that could become either a line of flight or line of articulation, depending on the alignment of directions followed by the assemblage: either parts of the assemblage move away from the main attractors, or on the contrary they all follow the same direction.

As a form of synthesis, we can propose a definition of transformation as *a deep redefinition of the space of possibility resulting from a reorientation of attractors and the emergence of new capacities*. In this context, the change of the properties of the assemblage can either be the origin or a consequence of the process. As we will develop in the next chapter, this conceptualisation of change suggests that we should spend less energy to control the actual capacities of assemblages and pay more attention to virtual capacities and attractors. Indeed, the former tends to concentrate all the resources in governance, while the latter is generally neglected. Governance should target attractors as much as the properties of the assemblage.

The subsequent sections discuss empirically how change and transformation are understood through the lens of assemblage thinking in our three cases. In Switzerland, we question the properties of the current agri-environmental governance (AEG) assemblage in relation to its capacities to overcome its limitations and produce meaningful transformations. Strongly rooted power relations seem to maintain a fundamental status quo, while allowing shallower processes of ecologisation. The centrality of logics of accountability and administrative control divert learning processes from a necessary co-construction of new agricultural and food knowledge. However, alternative processes of counter-power and knowledge creation lay the ground for the development of other possible futures. At the same time, ripple effects of small changes might reveal a stronger transformational dimension of the Swiss AEG, for instance in the case of a progressive restriction of pesticide uses. In the case of DS the different tools and actors that frame and articulate soya beans as part of a protein transition for Europe lay out the possibilities of an accelerated transformation that would affect substantially a whole range of areas in the food system. This case shows that a reconfiguration and its realisation depend to a great extent on making visible a number of small changes that interdependently impinge upon the physical and political infrastructures that are crucial to affecting change. As for RPPLH in

Indonesia, we highlight the properties and capacities of regulations, collaboration, and agri-environmental data. Big data has been particularly critical since its initial inception, where it became a scapegoat for the mismanagement of environmental governance in the country. NGOs blamed the government for the inaccuracies of environmental data presented to them, while the private sector was reluctant, and the state had been oblivious to collecting countrywide data. When the assemblage of actors agreed upon the importance of building data-driven environmental policies, the very nature of big data in fact altered the assemblage altogether. It reoriented actors towards new goals, restructured organisations, and reconfigured actors in the AEG assemblage. While big data, new forms of regulations, and collaboration indeed have the capacity to transform agri-food assemblages, it is by no means clear what kind of assemblage actors would be led to reimagine.

Small changes and the generation of attractors

As we have seen in Chapter 2, IP-Suisse emerged from a deep change in the Swiss AEG context in the 1990s. It reassembled agriculture and food actors according to new logics based on new power relations. The governance of agriculture moved from a state-centric model dominated by productivist values and objectives towards a multi-centric model that articulates liberal principles to environmental preoccupations. From an everyday approach, it played a role in reinforcing and stabilising new practices of governance that rely heavily on a logic of bureaucratisation and control. Through this, IP-Suisse has directly contributed to the transformation—defined as a reorientation of trajectories—of the previous dominant productivist and protectionist AEG assemblage, opening a new space of possibility. We also identified spaces of exploration and experimentation within the new assemblage. None of these experimentations was related to grand expectations in terms of transforming again the Swiss AEG assemblage as deeply as the previous political reform. Nevertheless, some of them had important effects in terms of what was seen as possible and feasible, reinforcing the idea that, from an assemblage perspective, small changes can have a dramatic impact on the long run through ripple effects that lead to a reconfiguration of relations in the assemblage. Those processes reshaped the assemblage by redefining its properties and reconfiguring its capacities to evolve in the future.

Let us come back to two examples already mentioned in the previous chapters, which allow us to consider the question of the potential and limitation of small changes: the example of a progressive ban on pesticide use in grain production and the development of a new value chain for Swiss quinoa.

The IP-Suisse standard for grain production already banned fungicides and insecticides in coordination with the "Extenso" scheme stemming from Switzerland's agricultural policy. Only herbicide use was tolerated before the germination of the crop in order to eradicate weeds. IP-Suisse conducted a first experiment on production without herbicide in collaboration with an industrial baker who wanted to offer bread made of zero-pesticide Swiss flour without having to deal with the complications of a fully organic value chain. All this happened at a time when the use of pesticides had been extensively discussed and criticised in political and media arenas. Indeed, the ban on (or very strong limitation of) pesticide use in agriculture was attacked by two "popular initiatives"—a kind of referendum that constitutes one of the instruments of Swiss direct democracy, allowing civil society to propose changes in the legislation. The campaign preceding the citizens' vote was intense and very conflictual. The two initiatives were rejected, but the intensity of the public debate on the topic could not be ignored.

In this context, IP-Suisse's main retail partner, Migros, was apparently inspired by the success of the aforementioned experiment. This trial in the real world of a flexible and trustworthy source of pesticide-free grain offered a very welcome opportunity to demonstrate one's commitment to sustainable agricultural production. In other words, the properties of the IP-Suisse assemblage that brings together and coordinates innovative farmers, industry partners, research institutions, and pre-existing practices of reducing pesticide use in wheat production opened up the way for different possible futures and new desires to emerge and converge in a shared direction. In parallel, the public debate on a potential ban on pesticides reinforced the idea of and the collective desire for a pesticide-free agriculture. In 2020, the retailer decided to integrate the new pesticide-free standard for the 85,000 tonnes of grain processed in its own bakery by 2023.

The experiment carried out by the farmer organisation IP-Suisse can be seen as a small step in a long chain of changes that happened notably in the selection of wheat varieties that are particularly resistant to disease and pests, in the successive adaptations of the federal agricultural policy, in the progressive establishment of the IP-Suisse standard, and in the evolution of retailers' strategies. However, obviously, IP-Suisse as an assemblage offered fertile ground for this kind of synergies and progressive developments. Many actors and elements of the assemblage contributed to the process, illustrating again the distributive nature of agency in assemblages, but more central to our point here is the convergence of desires leading the evolution of the IP-Suisse assemblage towards pesticide-free futures which became a strong attractor. As we have shown, many properties of the assemblage have been mobilised to produce new capacities towards such a future. Public debates, practical agricultural knowledge, and marketing strategies of differentiation have emerged and converged. This convergence of capacities and desires formed a new powerful attractor, which in turn oriented the desires of multiple actors in a similar direction, opening the space of possibility in a way that allows the IP-Suisse assemblage to evolve towards a pesticide-free future. The fact that a reduction of pesticide use in farm practices was from the beginning at the core of the IP-Suisse standard also explains this success: the new *pesticide-free future attractor* was quite aligned with the existing trajectory of the IP-Suisse assemblage. Its appearance in the basin of attraction did not involve major realignments of the relations making the assemblage.

Another example of an experiment initiated within the IP-Suisse assemblage is the development of the production of certified quinoa in Switzerland. In 2014, a few farmers, members of IP-Suisse, convinced the farmer organisation to back up their efforts to develop a full value chain for the regional production of quinoa. This initial support made it possible to mobilise the usual partners of IP-Suisse, notably a local mill and the retailer Migros. Thanks to the properties of the assemblage that gathers diverse competencies and infrastructures, technical and marketing issues could easily find first solutions. However, the new value chain did not really take off until now. Eight years after the launch of this regional production, the quinoa sold in Migros shops is still mostly imported under fair-trade and organic certifications. As for the regional production, it is only labelled with the guarantee of Swiss origin, without any specific environmental standard, which means without wearing the IP-Suisse "ladybird" label. Despite very positive coverage by the regional media who have told the "nice tale" of farmer entrepreneurship and innovation (Bétrisey, 2022), the regional IP-Suisse quinoa has not resulted in significant change at a large scale.

A few farmers were able to diversify their production and the shop of the local mill is now selling IP-Suisse quinoa products. Apparently, the *Swiss IP-Suisse certified quinoa attractor* was not strong enough. Despite the general success of local food, the capacity of farms to produce quinoa, and the support of many actors, the overall assemblage did not really follow this direction. Notably, the consumers apparently resisted the attraction. We have no clear explanation for this unsuccess to offer. However, it seems clear that the emerging production of IP-Suisse quinoa did not fit in well with the growing interest for new exotic crops like quinoa. Maybe the exotic identity of quinoa contrasted with the Swissness of the label. In any event, the convergence did not really happen.

In these two examples we see how small changes can easily develop in the IP-Suisse assemblage as long as they result in an alignment with the desires of key actors. The retailer wants to demonstrate its commitment to sustainability by showcasing the ban of pesticides in its bakeries? Then the IP-Suisse assemblage experimentation with pesticide-free grain production can spread and soon become the new norm for the label, as the retailer buys 80% of IP-Suisse grain. The farmer organisation wants to support new potential productions for its members and develop new markets, while the retailer sees synergies with its own strategy promoting regional products. Then the small group of farmers can launch a value chain for local quinoa and carve a new path for a more diverse agricultural production in the area. However, it is hard to identify ripple effects of these experimentations which would introduce deeper changes that could be called "transformative". Apparently, those seem rather small changes that led to a series of technical and relational adjustments, while remaining mostly within the frame of the existing material and immaterial territorialisation of the assemblage. In other words, these changes did not drastically modify the trajectory of the assemblage. On the contrary, they seem mostly to have reinforced the current configuration around the centrality of retailers and logics of certification. However, a more positive story can also be told, as valid as the former. These changes are still important and significant as they open new possibilities and directions for the next small changes that will inevitably happen: by rendering a large-scale, pesticide-free grain production beyond the organic niche concrete and thinkable; and by supporting processes of diversifying crops through the multiplication of small regional value chains.

The emergence of a protein transition as a new powerful attractor

In the previous chapter, we engaged with the constituting elements and "mechanics" that build attractors, thanks to meetings in the DS assemblage. In those spaces, governance aims and visions are being enacted through attracting desires in a collective that allows and enables reimaging, rethinking, and reframing desires towards a more integrated understanding of soya and the role it can play in a desirable protein transition in Europe. Within such framing, soya exhibits its capacity to reconfigure the ways in which protein plants and animal protein are used and made use of. The protein attractor emerges and finds a degree of stability in the basin of attraction forming around DS meetings and where the collective agency of the DS assemblage holds a determining role. The protein attractor enacts an imaginary of European agriculture based on more regional value chains, on improved trade relations between East and West, more productive soya crops, and the raising of quality for related grain and legume crops used for feed and food. These are imaginaries anchored in soya's capacity to produce ripple effects that catalyse a protein transition.

Attention to properties and capacities as elements of assemblages not only gives us a finer-grained view of the agencies at play that mobilise practices, desires, and goals but also a deeper grasp of the relationality between soya and protein that ultimately informs the atypical forms of change emerging from the DS organisation. Having an institutional setup that focuses on one crop alone to effect wider scale change in agricultural policies and practices is not the gold standard of reform in Europe's food systems, nor is it, as we show later, the silver-bullet measure of transformation. However, the assemblage approach provides us with perspectives on why and how this opens up new possibilities that are more desirable in terms of the sustainability of our food systems.

DS kept gaining momentum in a dynamic field nourished equally by tensions and alliances, or dynamics that Hodson et al. (2017) refer to as a mix of competing, coexisting, and complementary processes across domains and fields. In the case of DS, complementary processes create two trajectories that evolve synergistically to develop the political and economic conditions for soya on the one hand, and conditions for a protein transition on the other hand. Practices such as the creation of alliances with like-minded initiatives across the non-genetically modified (GM) organism markets, or partnerships with farmers, as well as tools such as a best-practice manual or the use of carbon-footprint assessments, feed the formation of the *sustainable/environmental soya attractor*. The everyday governance practice of meetings not only fully accommodates the environmental soya attractor in the basin of attraction but also feeds the emergence of the *protein-transition attractor*.

The concept of attractor enables us to provide alternative accounts of how transformation unfolds as well as how questions around assessments of AEG are reframed once potential understandings of future potentials are drawn out of the black box of dominant narratives. Moreover, attractors underline the possibility of seeing change occurring multi-directionally, of change occurring simultaneously across more than one domain or sector, or organisation, and of transformation occurring once one attractor gains in intensity, weakening the others that orbit in the larger assemblage. In this vein, some scenarios are losing traction, with business-as-usual models losing their grip on their critics and proponents alike, with fears of history repeating itself fading, and the shock of the new alleviated. In this sense, the attractors in the DS assemblage emerge as counterforces to the competing and coexisting forces shaping processes in the global soya assemblage. Forty different standards for soya beans occupy the economies of the soya sector. Global industry initiatives such as the Roundtable for Sustainable Soy, The Proterra Standard, and many others, converge with variously articulated soya criteria for responsible deforestation-free soya, along with feed manufacturers' associations and oil-processing industries in Europe. In the absence of a stronger legislative infrastructure, economic actors take the lead in developing more sustainable soya-based markets. While such standards compete on the European soya market with the DS standard, their gradual and growing take-up in the value chains does reinforce the demand for non-GM quality products, thereby weakening those aspects of the European Union's legislation on genetically modified organisms (GMOs) that allow inflows of GM soya for indirect consumption, such as in feed for livestock. The DS work on value-chain development and the attraction of retailers in support of specific qualities of soya, along with their contribution to a protein strategy, came to reveal new opportunities for addressing obstacles in the uptake of European soya. These do not just concern the European Union's policy of coexistence (between non-GM, GM, and organic) but also the excess of GM stipulations and standards, along with insufficient consideration of protein plants. However, expected protein policies and the harmonisation of GMO regulations have not yet actualised.

More recently, many of the concurring standards developed and gained traction around the emerging attractor of *sustainable meat*. Pressures to decarbonise the meat sector, and narratives forming around a collectively shared need to diminish meat consumption, cry out for the creation of new paths for change. Indeed, the meat industries are currently carving out possibilities for them transitioning to the production of plant-based products that mimic the texture and mouth-feel of meat. This experimentation phase and desire for technological innovation are backed up by consortia of actors worth multi-billion dollars. This new development presents DS with the possibility of further developing the network of stakeholders from the retail sector to take up certified European soya beans in their value chains, and thus further promoting the collaborations between those meat industries that are willing to transition to meat replacements and retailers, all the while strengthening the *sustainable meat attractor*. Much emphasis on the vegan markets was placed at the 2022 DS Conference in Vienna, with many European retailers showing enthusiasm and commitment to promote soya and thus further anchor the view of legume proteins as valuable for direct human consumption. These processes evolve as the socio-technical instruments for soya are being refined and made to work on the basis of the infrastructures created to move soya from East to West. The Ukrainian war showed the importance of physical infrastructures for facilitating soya at the same time that it brought new challenges in keeping to high standards, especially in terms of quality related to non-GMO and selective herbicide use. Lines of flight like those arriving with the Ukrainian war intervened only to confirm the need for improved, more diversified, and fitted adapted use of shipping systems by rail and by sea. The gradual developments that had supported the steady, albeit slow, certification of DS soya beans since 2012 proved helpful in lessening the fragility of food chains in the advent of crises and severe disruptions. The desire expressed by DS (through the Legume Transition proposal of 2016) to the European Union for the inclusion of a value-chain approach in the Directorate for Agriculture's plans and strategies on economic relations between East and West was eventually realised independently of decisions missed in this respect at EU level. Nonetheless, the European Union's decision to support Legume Translated, a new project started in 2018, was actualised in the creation of a knowledge and exchange platform—Legume Hub—intended to promote in a unique way flows of technical knowledge and innovation for practitioners. While such developments were welcomed, the expected integration of value-chain approaches to support East-to-West flows (as demanded in the Legume Transition document from 2016) did not actualise.

This is anything but a stall, for the assemblage is multiplying relations with new networks and projects spreading from the initial conditions carved out by the DS assemblage. Since 2019, new developments have pointed to potentials that could contribute to the actualisation of a protein assemblage. New initiatives and associations were created around Europe. These exist as independent entities from DS, though they may include DS advisors in their boards, or are in the process of becoming established as their ideas and plans take on. They include Fields of Europe (formally established in 2021 as a standard to integrate food and feed, extending beyond soya to other grains used to produce proteins); the European Non-GM Industry Association (established in 2019; it highlights and represents the business interests of national non-GM industries and economic operators (production, processing, marketing, retail, certification, labelling) vis-à-vis the political bodies of the European Union); the Collaborative Soy Initiative (established in 2019; the focus lies on communications and actions that promote synergies between stakeholders); and the European National Soya Initiative (established in 2021 to identify issues of common interest in the field of sustainability, international trade, and European affairs where these relate directly to soya production, and to exchange good practices between the national soya initiatives). Far from being a flat and fragmented multiplication of initial conditions, the assemblage grows rhizomatically (Deleuze & Guatarri, 1988). Relations with actors are extended to support the non-GM market, including the meat sector and forest conservation, the policy environment, the sustainable development of other crops, and the sense-making processes for soya across economic borders. In this vein, assemblages thrive on heterogeneity and on more than one attractor, lending intensity to the *protein transition attractor* and accelerating the orbiting speed of the *environmental soya attractor.*

Transformative pathways and the spectrum of possibilities

The previous chapters have highlighted how the Indonesian government, academics, and community groups put high hopes on RPPLH as a planning instrument that might change whole practices of environmental governance. Amidst the ever-changing environmental governance landscapes in the country, this instrument could lead to something more than change—a complete transformation. It was supposed to restructure the planning, permit-granting, monitoring, and evaluation processes into something that places the environment at the centre of calculation. It would lock areas and regions according to their predesignated purposes, be they agricultural production, industrial complex, or conservation and protection. It would close down unnecessary business negotiations and redirect development according to what the government wants, preferably on the basis of sustainable development goals.

Over the course of more than a decade since a new environmental management law was enacted in 2009, none of these hopes came to fruition. Development was still guided by the so-called business as usual in which environmental assessments were made subsequently as a response to proposed development projects, although new instruments such as the Strategic Environmental Assessment (*Kajian Lingkungan Hidup Strategis*, KLHS) have begun to take shape. Regional and provincial governments across Indonesia have now engaged more frequently with RPPLH, through training, courses, assistance, and consultancy work with experts and academics. Some have even succeeded in preparing a formal RPPLH document that the ministry would approve, although the implementation of this planning document is a different story altogether. National strategic projects, such as hydroelectric dams or high-speed railways, still run their course regardless of any RPPLHs. The general public is most likely still oblivious to what RPPLH is.

We can therefore be fairly sure that transformation does not transpire in the case of RPPLH, as no major reorientation of the Indonesian AEG assemblage can be directly observed. To put it more clearly, transformation as a "project" (Forney & Dwiartama, 2023), as it is imagined by the decision-makers and planners, has been a failure. Explicit goals that are embedded within the idea of transformation may not be achieved; changes, however, do happen. As in the case of IP-Suisse and DS, ripple effects from little changes may lead to a certain unexpected pathway. These changes can at least open up multiple possibilities, for better or worse. If we refrain from looking at transformation as a form of intentionality, then we may be able to see beyond success and failure, which leads us to a different understanding of *change*. Assemblage thinking carries a radical understanding of change in which strategic action and unintentional effects and reconfigurations combine in leading actors to navigate a new set of assemblages.

To illustrate this, we bring three examples of what the small changes that RPPLH made led to or aligned with. The first is a simplification of environmental permits. As mentioned in Chapter 2, development projects in Indonesia relied on rigorous, painstaking environmental permits on the basis of AMDAL, or Environmental Impact Assessments. Depending on the scale of the industry, a company needs to develop an environmental assessment that identifies every stage of the development project and the potential impacts of each of the stages on the local community and environment, including the mitigation and monitoring plans in regard to those impacts. The process requires not only a thorough study but also a series of public hearings to ensure that the result is communicated transparently to community members. The consecutive processes would then be assessed by the environmental agency and a third-party reviewer for a decision on the permit to be made. Loopholes are usually present in every stage of the process, be it an AMDAL consultant not reporting the correct data, a public hearing being untransparent, or an official being bribed to release a permit. What complicates the matter is that the permit given to a company often ignores the opportunity cost of developing something else in the area. An agricultural agency official, for instance, lamented about the declining agricultural area because more and more permits were given to the construction of manufacturing factories.

When RPPLH was introduced, it offered a breath of fresh air to the pressing land-use-change problems, by assigning a designated function to a piece of land. As we understand, the scheme has not been implemented consistently. Still, a partial manifestation of its fundamental logic surprisingly lingers: administrative simplification. In 2021, the national government introduced the 1,187-page Omnibus Bill (Law Number 11 of 2020; see Sembiring et al., 2020: 1) with one specific aim, "… to deregulate the scattered, overlapping, and disharmonious laws related to business activities in Indonesia", or, put simply, to ease developing business in the country. The Bill amended 78 other laws and 1,288 articles, including the 2009 Environmental Protection and Management Law (the one which mandated the use of RPPLH). Although the obligation of the central, provincial, and regional governments to formulate and implement RPPLH is still present, what changes in the Omnibus Bill is the way the environmental permit is weakened and replaced by a broader business permit, which contains an environmental approval. This transition towards a more simplified environmental due diligence aligns with the spirit of RPPLH, in which what is necessary is the compliance of a given business development project with the regional spatial planning, which further complies with the environmental planning as stated in RPPLH. Yet, there is a notable sliding in the direction leading to this simplification, from an environment-centred to a business-centred logic. The change of terminology from "permit" to "approval", amidst the vague and premature RPPLH, is perhaps one of the factors that created backlashes and protests among environmental activists. This notwithstanding, we would argue that, on the one hand, RPPLH has opened, or justified, one new pathway of environmental governance in Indonesia. On the other hand, we see the emergence of a *centralisation of control on the basis of ease-of-doing-business attractor* that acts on the RPPLH assemblage and imposes its trajectory.

The second small change that RPPLH introduced is a new form of collaboration in doing planning. Prior to RPPLH, planning was mainly done from the top down, according to the political agenda and programmes of the elected governors, majors, or regents. With the introduction of RPPLH, the ministry could now implement a stricter rule on planning: after a governor/major/regent is inaugurated, his/ her administration must compile an RPPLH over the next six months, otherwise some part of their budget would be withheld. This leads to the formation of a task force that consists of representatives from different agencies working together on the said document. Consultants are often invited but data, reports, analyses, and decisions are all made by the task force. This is a relatively new approach to planning. Previously, the Planning Agency played a central role, whereas other agencies provided only inputs. Now, a more distributed and collaborative planning seems to take shape, regardless of whether the RPPLH itself is successful or not. We can say that RPPLH helped to introduce changes in the properties of land-use governance, particularly by changing the way agencies relate to each other. As discussed more in depth in Chapter 4, this environmental planning scheme has brought a new pathway for governing sideways and across sectors. In this sense, we might consider that a *cross-sectoral collaboration attractor* has been predominant in the case of RPPLH.

This relates to the third attractor, which relates to data-driven governance (Hughes et al., 2020). RPPLH has brought something new to the table which is data, or to be more precise, a new way of looking at data. While data, and particularly ecological data, were also considered in previous spatial and development planning, they were never truly the central aspect that mobilised strategies and decisions. RPPLH not only helps in expanding the range and scope of data used in decision-making but also pushes for a more accurate and detailed set of data. For example, in order to simulate a projected population growth and the consequences for waste production, water consumption, and land-use change, the RPPLH task force must have collected time-series data on the population and its spatial distribution, along with the amount of household waste produced on average, average water *needs per capita*, and many other environmental indicators. The richer the data, the more accurate the projection is supposed to be. These projections would then be used as part of a decision-support tool to determine the most sustainable use of areas and regions.

In advocating for this richer set of data, some agencies offered ways to engage with the idea of "big data" in their respective sectors. The Ministry of Agriculture, for instance, installed weather-monitoring stations on a few sites to build a more accurate climate prediction. The Ministry of Trade collects prices of major agricultural commodities on the central markets on a weekly basis and provides the data to the wider public through a web portal. Environmental agencies in major cities place air-quality-monitoring panels in central business districts and show the numbers to the general public in real time. In West Java, each agency develops its own platforms for their information systems, one for each form of data (village potentials, farmers' groups, epidemiology, market prices, soil properties, land suitability for crop production, etc.), although we would argue that these platforms have not been able to demonstrate the richness and variability of data. This convergence of actions towards the production of increasing and more precise data reflects the influence of a common attractor, *the promises of Big Data attractor*, which RPPLH helped to consolidate and anchor in the Indonesian context. This is different from the way in which data were used before the ubiquity of digital technology (see, e.g. Kitchin, 2014).

The increasing trend towards big data is captured not only by government offices but also, and arguably more effectively, by local communities (as in the case of farmers' groups collecting rainfall data; see

Winarto et al., 2018) and start-ups (see, e.g. Forney & Dwiartama, 2023). Some agri-food startups, for instance, collaborate with the provincial government in providing user-collected data on pests and diseases, water quality, crop yields, and market prices. Their collected dataset is a form of trade-off with farmers, who gain benefits from the free use of those companies' apps/technologies, which can then be used to predict market trends and meet offtakers' demands for agricultural products. At the same time, these startups also reap benefits from their involvement with government projects, or as simple as being endorsed by the government (which for them means a huge potential for scalability). Reciprocally, most often they would provide the government with their collected data for the latter to monitor programmes or, more likely, to claim success in achieving targets.

This engagement with big data or collaborative planning was by no means initiated by RPPLH. Collaborative planning has been the spirit of governance—and a strong attractor—during the post-reform era and particularly after the 2014 Bill on Regional Autonomy (Undang Undang Republik Indonesia Nomor 23, 2014) giving the regional and provincial governments broader responsibilities in key development aspects. Likewise, big data became an integral part of the terminology of the public sector around 2018 without any connection to environmental planning. If anything, it was probably big data that later influenced how RPPLH-related policy was designed. However, RPPLH as an assemblage aligns perfectly with the ubiquitous data and their everyday use. It opens up the possibility of planning, managing, and monitoring the environment on the basis of data, together with the heterogeneous elements that come with it (communities, companies, startups, academics, devices, apps, and platforms). Along with collaborative planning, RPPLH demonstrates the capacity to produce new kinds of environmental governance in Indonesia. Particularly to the conceptual framework surrounding AEG as assemblage, this case provides an example of how governance can be seen as something beyond policies, planning, and regulations, and more as relationships, configurations, and anticipations of multiple possibilities.

Concluding remarks: a radical understanding of change

This chapter has highlighted what change and transformation are through the lens of assemblage thinking. Change is associated with unpredictability and multi-linearity, but also with the properties and capacities of the very assemblage to manifest into many different possibilities. Some of these capacities (such as pesticide-free policies, meat alternatives, or data-driven governance) might be more desirable than others, relevant to different assemblages, and strong enough to move an assemblage towards a new future direction. We identify this form of capacities and their ramification with other assemblages as attractors. By understanding this, we can safely say that an assemblage, despite leading to multiple and often unpredictable changes, is not necessarily chaotic. We may return to talk about transformation, for instance, as something that we aim to pursue, as a change of direction, but while also being aware that it may lead to some unexpected places.

What this implies for our understanding of AEG is that we might need to recognise the diversity of alternatives and future trajectories (Gibson-Graham & Dombroski, 2020) and to navigate away from the idea of stability in order to emphasise the multiplicity of assemblages as always-becoming. Assemblage thinking is a radical understanding of change where transformation is not considered in opposition to stability but instead to other changes, and where diverse directions of change can coexist. Over the course of this book, we have emphasised repeatedly that adopting assemblage thinking brings a deep shift in how we think about unpredictability, multiple possibilities, agency, power, and now, change and stability.

This way of thinking, of course, is not exclusive to academics, but extends to practitioners and decision-makers as well. We argue that assemblage thinking is useful not only in how we interpret the world but also, and more importantly, in how we change it, "by introducing transformative thinking into the relationship to the present" (Braidotti, 2019: 465). To refer to Castree et al. (2021), there is a need for a politics turn towards wicked assessments, a wider range of worldviews, and productive dissensus. In Saldanha's (2012: 197) view, the "so what" question can be answered by assemblage thinking to "disturb hegemonic desire! to better intervene!". In Chapter 6, we will explore what assemblage thinking means in the practical sphere of AEG.

Notes

1 www.un.org/en/food-systems-summit/about, last accessed 27.09.2023.
2 www.worldbank.org/en/programs/food-systems-2030/food-systems-tra nsformation, last accessed 27.09.2023.

3 We will revisit this notion of stability with a similar concept in assemblage thinking, namely, basins of attraction, later in this chapter.
4 Gunderson and Holling have proposed this idea of panarchy (Gunderson & Holling, 2002), which is based on Holling's (1973) seminal work on stability and resilience in ecological systems.

References

Barnett, V. (1998). *Kondratiev and the Dynamics of Economic Development.* London: Macmillan.
Bennett, J. (2010). *Vibrant Matter: A Political Ecology of Things.* Durham and London: Duke University Press.
Bétrisey, F. (2022). Récit médiatique de la production de quinoa en Suisse: idéalisation du local et dépolitisation de l'agriculture. *Géo-Regards* 15: 125–142.
Braidotti, R. (2019). Affirmative ethics and generative life. *Deleuze and Guattari Studies* 13(4): 463–481.
Callon, M. (1984). Some elements of a sociology of translation: Domestication of the scallops and the fishermen of St Brieuc Bay. *The Sociological Review*, 32(1_suppl): 196–233.
Castree, N., Bellamy, R., & Osaka, S. (2021). The future of global environmental assessments: making a case for fundamental change. *The Anthropocene Review* 8(1): 56–82.
Deleuze, G., & Guatarri, F. (1988). *A Thousand Plateaus: Capitalism and Schizophrenia.* London: Athlone.
Dittmer, J. (2014). Geopolitical assemblages and complexity. *Progress in Human Geography* 38(3): 385–401.
Dwiartama, A. (2017). Resilience and transformation of the New Zealand kiwifruit industry in the face of Psa-V disease. *Journal of Rural Studies* 52: 118–126.
Folke, C., Carpenter, S., Elmqvist, T., Gunderson, L., Holling, C. S., & Walker, B. (2002). Resilience and sustainable development: building adaptive capacity in a world of transformations. *AMBIO: A Journal of the Human Environment* 31(5): 437–440.
Forney, J., & Dwiartama, A. (2023). The project, the everyday, and reflexivity in sociotechnical agri-food assemblages: proposing a conceptual model of digitalisation. *Agriculture and Human Values* 40(2): 441–454.
Foster, J. B. (1999). Marx's theory of metabolic rift: classical foundations for environmental sociology. *American Journal of Sociology* 105(2): 366–405.
Geels, F. W. (2007). Transformations of large technical systems: a multilevel analysis of the Dutch highway system (1950–2000). *Science, Technology, & Human Values* 32(2): 123–149.

Geels, F. W. (2010). Ontologies, socio-technical transitions (to sustainability), and the multi-level perspective. *Research Policy* 39(4): 495–510.

Gibson-Graham, J.-K., & Dombroski, K. (2020). *The Handbook of Diverse Economies*. Cheltenham and Northampton: Edward Elgar Publishing.

Gunderson, L. H., & Holling, C. S. (Eds.). (2002). *Panarchy: Understanding Transformations in Human and Natural Systems*. Washington, D.C.: Island Press.

Hodson, M., Geels, F. W., & McMeekin, A. (2017). Reconfiguring urban sustainability transitions, analysing multiplicity. *Sustainability* 9(2): 299.

Holling, C. S. (1973). Resilience and stability of ecological systems. *Annual Review of Ecology and Systematics* 4(1): 1–23.

Hughes, S., Giest, S., & Tozer, L. (2020). Accountability and data-driven urban climate governance. *Nature Climate Change* 10(12): 1085–1090.

Jansen, K. (2015). The debate on food sovereignty theory: agrarian capitalism, dispossession and agroecology. *The Journal of Peasant Studies* 42(1): 213–232.

Jarosz, L. (2014). Comparing food security and food sovereignty discourses. *Dialogues in Human Geography* 4(2): 168–181.

Kitchin, R. (2014). Big Data, new epistemologies and paradigm shifts. *Big Data & Society* 1(1): 2053951714528481.

Magarini, A., & Porreca, E. (2019). *European Cities Leading in Urban Food Systems Transformation: Connecting Milan & FOOD 2030*. Luxembourg: Publications Office of the European Union.

Protevi, J. (2006). Deleuze, Guattari and Emergence. *Paragraph* 29(2): 19–39.

Rip, A. (2006). A co-evolutionary approach to reflexive governance – and its ironies. In V. Jan-Peter, D. Bauknecht, & R. Kemp (Eds.). *Reflexive Governance for Sustainable Development* (pp. 82–100). Cheltenham, UK/ Northampton, MA: Edward Elgar.

Saldanha, A. (2012). Assemblage, materiality, race, capital. *Dialogues in Human Geography* 2(2): 194–197.

Scott, D. (2011). The Technological fix criticisms and the agricultural biotechnology debate. *Journal of Agricultural and Environmental Ethics* 24(3): 207–226.

Sembiring, R., Fatimah, I., & Widyaningsih, G. A. (2020). Indonesia's omnibus bill on job creation: a setback for environmental law?. *Chinese Journal of Environmental Law* 4(1): 97–109.

Stirling, A. (2015). Emancipating Transformations: from controlling 'the transition' to culturing plural radical progress. In I. Scoones, M. Leach, & P. Newell (Eds.). *The Politics of Green Transformations* (pp. 54–67). New York and London: Routledge.

Undang Undang Republik Indonesia Nomor 23. (2014). Tentang Pemerintahan Daerah (*Law on Regional Governments*).

Walker, B., Carpenter, S. R., Rockstrom, J., Crépin, A. S., & Peterson, G. D. (2012). Drivers, "slow" variables, "fast" variables, shocks, and resilience. *Ecology and Society* 17(3): 30.

Walker, B., Holling, C. S., Carpenter, S. R., & Kinzig, A. (2004). Resilience, adaptability and transformability in social–ecological systems. *Ecology and Society* 9(2): 5.

Walker, B., Gunderson, L., Kinzig, A., Folke, C., Carpenter, S., & Schultz, L. (2006). A handful of heuristics and some propositions for understanding resilience in social–ecological systems. *Ecology and Society* 11(1): 13.

Winarto, Y. T., Ariefiansyah, R., Prihandiani, A. F., & Taqiuddin, M. (2018). Nurturance and trust in developing agrometeorological learning in a changing climate: the science field shops in Indonesia. *Indonesia and the Malay World* 46(136): 360–381.

6 Governing emergence towards the transformation of agri-food assemblages

Introduction: from reflexive governance to governance of emergence

The ways agri-environmental governance (AEG) is currently thought of and conceptualised in reorienting and transforming our food systems towards more desirable and sustainable futures seem to be bound for failure. Assemblage theory, in dialogue with empirical work on everyday AEG, opens new perspectives for dealing with some of the classical conundrums of governance studies. This core idea is at the basis of this book and triggered the conceptual developments in every chapter. After setting the scene and introducing our approach and project in the introduction, we started by framing empirical case studies (Chapter 2) from an everyday-governance perspective. Over and above individualised instruments, complex and entangled governance assemblages have appeared. Those assemblages are not well-defined and stabilised systems. They are sets of concrete relations between heterogeneous elements, and these relations transgress the usual categories used to qualify governance. Assemblages are traversed by destabilising tensions (lines of flight) and forces of cohesion (lines of articulation). In this sense, AEG assemblages and the relations that made them are always changing and recreated. They are vibrant (Bennett, 2010) and always becoming. The intricacy of the relations making an assemblage and the diverse forces that traverse them inevitably generate a diversity and multiplicity of processes.

Assemblage is defined by what they produce (Buchanan, 2021), and this multiplicity of outcomes, found at the level of desires, imaginaries, or material processes, is a core feature of assemblage thinking. This is what we understand when Deleuze and Guattari define assemblage as

DOI: 10.4324/9781003271260-6

being, at the same time, one and many. More concretely, the same AEG assemblage can result in diverse, sometimes contradictory, outcomes. It can simultaneously nurture practices of bureaucratic control and stimulate environmental experimentation at its margins. This multiplicity of outcomes also means that predicting them is challenging. What resulted from a governance action was always, at least partly, unexpected. This observation opens a new question about assessing the outcomes of governance practices (Chapter 3). Their fundamental unpredictability forces us to think beyond success or failure, and to pay more attention to the unintended effects of governance. Indeed, what emerges from AEG assemblages is often quite distant from stated objectives and goals. Interventions change the configuration of the assemblage, indirectly impacting its elements and their relations. The apparent failure of a new governance scheme can still be productive in transforming the way governance actors, such as state offices and services, relate to one another. Therefore, governance can also be seen as an attempt to ride this uncertainty rather than setting objectives and assessing achievements.

Unpredictability does not mean that actors have absolutely no capacity to orient what AEG assemblages become. On the contrary, the questions of agency and power are not only central to the topic of governance itself but also to an assemblage approach (Chapter 4). However, to understand better the capacity of elements to influence the course of an assemblage, one must accept to move away from an individualistic definition of agency and integrate its collective and distributive nature. No one acts alone in an assemblage.

Power can take many forms, some being ephemeral and others well-established, depending on how consolidated relations in the assemblage are. Therefore, voluntary or circumstantial alliances are essential in the capacity of individual elements to act according to their interest or will. What makes assemblages hold together is the coming together of desires. Joint interests create powerful movements in the assemblage, orienting its future evolutions. From this perspective, the emergence of shared desires and projects, for instance, around a redefinition of the role of soya in European agriculture is a central aspect of the collective agency of AEG assemblages and points to their capacity to impinge on broader food and agriculture assemblages.

This discussion on agency and power then leads us to the question of social change and transformation, which stands as AEG's fundamental objective (Chapter 5). As a starting point, assemblages' vibrant and always-in-becoming nature emphasises the mundanity of change. What matters then is not so much "changing" things, but rather understanding which change counts and how it is located within a broader direction of changes. Transforming food and agriculture becomes a matter of changing the general directions guiding the assemblage. In this process, small changes can become meaningful when they contribute to the emergence of new attractors and the creation of new spaces of possibilities. Altogether, assemblage thinking provides useful tools for a renewed and regenerated engagement with AEG in a context where "transformation" is called for by many actors.

In this final and concluding chapter, we build an argument that assemblage thinking can participate in the much-needed transformation of our agri-food systems. Laying the emphasis on the notion of emergence and capacities, assemblage thinking contributes to a paradigmatic change and an epistemological turn in how we address unpredictability in the practice of governance. The articulation of individual, collective, and distributive agency and the related attention paid to the multiplicity of ongoing processes of change are not only useful framings for analysing power relations and the effects of governance but can also help to recalibrate the way we develop and target new governance instruments, and to nurture crucial transformative processes which are premised on the reordering of power relations to overcome locked-in situations. The everyday perspective on governance usefully helps to redefine and go beyond the notion of reflexivity in governance. The distributive nature of agency in governance assemblages critically questions the focus on "governing" in steering governance practices, neglecting the need for a more distributed reflexivity in the whole assemblage.

As already stated, assemblage thinking provides useful tools for scrutinising unwanted effects and spillovers. Therefore, and leaving academic considerations aside, it is a useful guide in the practice of governance for building reflexive and transformative assemblages of instruments, by targeting capacities and attractors, as leverage points, rather than specific objectives that will always remain elusive and fundamentally unachievable. Thus, we claim that assemblage thinking makes a double contribution to the debates surrounding AEG. The first is to show how assemblage theory is useful in understanding issues around governance. The second is the promotion of a practice of governance that would focus on creating new assemblages as a powerful tool of change. This last chapter engages more directly with this second contribution by asking questions such as: What does it mean to leave aside a definition of governance as steering, based on objectives and monitoring, or on the success and failure of assessment? Can we do governance without fixed objectives? How can ripple effects and small changes be integrated to govern "sideways" without necessarily belittling our ambitions? What does "embracing uncertainty" mean concretely? Simply put, this final chapter serves as a first translation of the book's theoretical contributions into a vocabulary more attuned to the needs of the actors of governance, such as policymakers, NGOs, or local food organisations.

The unruly consequences of governance and the call for reflexive governance

As presented in the introductory chapter of this book, our original inspiration for engaging in this discussion on everyday governance and AEG assemblages can be found in our previous engagement with AEG practices. There, we worked to identify several weaknesses and limitations in how our current societies develop answers to agri-environmental issues and challenges. Of course, this statement also builds on what many authors have said in a large literature addressing AEG practices' many failures, weaknesses, and unwanted effects. The rich body of scholarship emphasises once again that, as unpredictable assemblages, governance practices rarely reach only the expected results. The extreme difficulty of predicting evolutions and developments is a key feature of complexity thinking, and this is particularly true for matters of sustainability. Many factors mingle and render the governance of socio-ecological transformation unpredictable: hidden abodes, external interventions, fortuitous interactions and events, and diverse forms of resistance (e.g. Voß & Kemp, 2006). Because of these difficulties in achieving explicit goals, Miller and Rose (1990) speak of the idea of "government" as a "congenitally failing operation". Consequently, they claim, the "will to govern" needs to be understood "in terms of the difficulties of operationalising it", as the unruly nature of social life can never be fully captured by any form of knowledge that informs governing programmes (ibid.: 10–11). Therefore, as Walker and Shove (2007: 222) argue, contingencies and ambivalences in pursuing governance objectives must be seen as "a normal rather than a pathological state".

Despite these already old critical assessments, the design of governance interventions, in the overwhelming majority of cases, remains based on simplification and schematisation that translate into monolinear anticipation of change. This may be explained using Scott's (1998) insight that "seeing like a state" systematically requires certain forms of knowledge and control based on oversimplification. This narrowing of the vision makes possible imaginations of rigorous control, accurate measurement, and precise manipulation of an otherwise far too complex and unwieldy reality. Shove (2010) already highlighted that criticising such a linear and simplistic vision is not limited to the theoretical debate, but has concrete implications as they produce a "template for intervention" that attributes specific roles to diverse actors and closes different possibilities of action. From a different perspective, an everyday and assemblage approach to governance renders such simplifications unbearable, as no one lives in a world where issues can be fully isolated and separately resolved. Multiplicity, unpredictability, and perpetual change are not only key elements of a theory of assemblages; they also reflect the everyday experience of actors involved in governance practice. Too often, the failure of governance interventions is explained by the actors' resistance or the task's difficulty. This critical analysis of simplification in governance tells us that the cause of failure might just as well be found on the side of the theory of change and the templates for intervention in which governance instruments are produced. Indeed, Shove (2010: 1278) also highlights that "effect is never in isolation and that interventions go on within, not outside, the processes they seek to shape", pointing to the need for governance actors to see themselves as part of the "system that they have to govern" (Rip, 2006: 82), which also means assuming part of the responsibility for the outcomes.

These observations rejoin calls for a careful and reflexive practice of governance, as formulated by Voß and Kemp:

Reflexive governance refers to the problem of shaping societal development in the light of the reflexivity of steering strategies— the phenomenon that thinking and acting with respect to an object of steering also affects the subject and its ability to steer. Examples of such reflexivity include research policies bringing up new knowledge that shifts policy objectives, or subsidies increasing the lobbying power of supported industries and thereby changing political force fields. Reflexive governance thus implies that one calls into question the foundations of governance itself, that is, the concepts, practices and institutions by which societal development is governed, and that one envisions alternatives and reinvents and shapes those foundations.

(Voß and Kemp, 2006: 4)

The idea of nurturing reflexivity among the actors of governance is not limited to the literature on "reflexive governance" and can be found in the work of many scholars. In general, this literature includes more concrete recommendations. For instance, in the conclusion to his critical engagement with development policies and their continuous failure, Scott (1998: 345) provides a few rules of thumb "to make development planning less prone to disaster". First, because we cannot predict the future and remain largely ignorant of what will come next, caution and small steps should be the rule to avoid irremediable negative consequences. As the author puts it: "a small step, stand back, observe and then plan the next small move". Second, and as part of the same logic, governance action should favour reversibility. Third, one should plan for a surprise and be prepared to accommodate his/her actions to the unforeseen. Fourth, one should also plan for human inventiveness and the capacity of actors to play with the rules. James Scott's recommendations emerge from his work on development policies and programmes in Africa. Nevertheless, they find a strong echo in Alejandro Portes's 1999 presidential address to the American Sociological Association on unpredictability, when he called for more cautious policy interventions:

These alternative forms require relentless questioning of the initial blueprints and an examination of the various contingencies at each step of program implementation. In particular, this approach results in two practical considerations: First, change must proceed in measured steps, with close attention to fortuitous events and pressures from outside forces; second, one must know the actors involved and their actual goals in order to anticipate their reactions to external intervention.

(2000: 14–15)

The core of reflexive governance is creating conditions that allow continuous attention to the "unforeseen" or the "fortuitous", as opposed to usual practices of governance where all the efforts concentrate on the construction of strong and well-thought-out instruments, with few resources left for serious monitoring and reassessment of the intervention. As Walker and Shove put it:

> A system orientation when combined with ideas of reflexive governance consequently implies not one moment of intervention, following which managers stand back and await the desired result, but a constant process in which further adjustments are made as environmental conditions change, these changes being, in part, the outcome of previous interventions. Feedback, monitoring and circuits of action and reaction are integral to this overall scheme.
>
> (2007: 219)

The assemblage approach we developed in the previous chapter partly leads to similar conclusions. Notably, the emphasis on the unpredictability of outcomes in AEG assemblages strongly echoes the idea of the unforeseen and the fortuitous mentioned by these scholars. However, "reflexive governance" alone, as an alternative framework, does not fully engage with some of the questions assemblage thinking raises on AEG practices, which include, among others, the multiplicity of outcomes, the distributive nature of agency, the non-linearity of change, and the existence of attractors. Scott and Portes might have touched upon some of those aspects without fully integrating them. Assemblage thinking, we argue, gives us the means to go beyond reflexive governance, which appears as a first and important step on a longer way towards a more profound and articulated reconfiguration of the principles of doing governance.

The limitations of reflexivity and the need to embrace emergences

Reflexive governance is essentially based on a feedback-loop model. This model can translate into a series of steps following a "formulation–implementation–reformulation" sequence. While such a model introduces more complexity and forces us to pay attention to the unexpected effects of interventions, it preserves a form of linearity in the definition of governance goals as the unique direction of change and the multiplicity of outcomes being reduced to mere side effects that should be avoided if unwanted. Also, reflexive governance remains centred around the original intention of the actors of governance. This argument is mobilised in the controversy between assemblage theorists, when Buchanan criticises DeLanda's position on the reflexive model (even if none of these authors calls it that). Buchanan (2021: 125) makes an important comment based on the concept of intentional fallacy: "This way of seeing policy succumbs to what literary theorists refer to as the 'intentional fallacy' because it holds to the idea that a policy can and should be measured against a policy intention". Buchanan introduces the notion of wild policy he borrows from Lea (2014) to counter the idea that policies (and governance at large, we would add) are controllable processes guided by intentions and precise plans, which is more an image that policies produce of themselves than an accurate reflection of the messiness of real life. The wild side of policies described by Lea relates explicitly to criticism of Australian liberalism and does not overlap exactly with our theorisation of AEG assemblages, despite the wilderness of governance also expressing itself in the notion of multiplicity and distributive agency. This contradicts the centrality of individual intentions and points to the fundamentally uncontrollable nature of what emerges from assemblages following governance interventions.

The insistence on the wild dimension of governance has both an analytical and a practical value. On the one hand, we hope to have demonstrated in this book that governance is better understood when described as an assemblage. On the other hand, as Stirling (2015) puts it, the enormous challenges our societies face today demand moving away from an illusion of control through governance. The author opposes emancipating transformations to shallower transitions; the first "involving more diverse, emergent and unruly political alignments, more about social innovations, challenging incumbent structures, subject to incommensurable knowledge and pursuing contending (even unknown) ends", and the latter being "managed under orderly control, through incumbent structures according to tightly disciplined knowledge, often emphasising technological innovation, towards some particular known (presumptively shared) end" (ibid.: 54). Following a similar inspiration, our purpose here is to emphasise the need to go beyond "reflexive governance", which tends to maintain an ontology of change as linear and controllable, adding a layer of caution and attention in the process. Instead, we propose the basis for a *governance of emergence* that acknowledges the multiplicity and messiness of change and the challenges brought by the distributive nature of agency. In the following, we do so by identifying and sketching out four guiding principles.

Redistributing responsibilities

In the introduction to a recent special issue on "Governing Food Futures: Towards a 'Responsibility Turn' in Food and Agriculture", Arnold and colleagues (2022) discuss the "turn to responsibility" in the governance of agri-food systems, highlighting the centrality of power relations in the attribution of responsibilities. Even if its proximity with neoliberal discourses is pertinently criticised, the notion of responsibility itself remains central in governance, as it guides action by defining who has to respond to problems. The authors highlight this process of responsibilisation as "a 'constitution of the self' of the actors of the system in relation to a common set of rules or norms" (ibid.: 83). In other words, responsibilisation calls upon the—voluntary or not—engagement of all the reflexive elements of an assemblage in acknowledging their share of responsibility for what emerges from the assemblage. The process of taking or attributing responsibility inevitably raises the question of power relations—some actors can avoid responsibility, while others have to take a larger share of it than they might deserve. The combination of individual, collective, and distributive agency—highlighted in assemblage thinking—helps reframe this ambivalence of responsibilisation. Maye and colleagues (2019) highlight the limitations of individual responsibilisation in solving large-scale and systemic issues, echoing the call for "more collective notions of responsibility and the acknowledgment that *responsibilities are distributed* across complex networks of actors" (ibid.: 303). To this end, they draw on, among others, Barnett and colleagues' (2011) definition of responsibility as

> not just an individuated action taken by a single person or by some collective agent. It is theorised in terms of how distributed actions join actors together, feeding into wider networks of cooperation that reach out and influence events elsewhere.
> (Barnett et al., 2011, cited in Maye et al., 2019: 303)

Evans and colleagues (2017: 1401) identified "an emergent sense of distributed responsibility" in the framing of food-waste-reduction actions by supermarkets in the United Kingdom, not without interrogating what such powerful actors renounced to divert responsibility towards other actors. Their work calls for caution in the idealisation of distributed responsibility as a tool for diluting responsibility.

A *governance of emergence* combines a distributed understanding of responsibility—echoing the distributive agency—with a critical engagement with power relations as a key issue in making the transition possible through a "reassignment of rights and responsibilities" (Sareen & Wolf, 2021: 2)—reflecting the power dynamics in assemblages. As stated, taking seriously the distributive nature of agency does not equal ignoring the unequal distribution of power to influence the course of the assemblage. On the contrary, distributive agency calls for a redistribution of responsibilities according to the capacity of elements to act on the wider assemblage. In simple words, more power implies more responsibility in the collective outcomes.

In the case of IP-Suisse, the significant development of pesticide-free grain production resulted from a distributed set of actions and self-responsibilisation. Civil society, retailers, research institutions, farmer organisations, state agencies, and individuals all brought their contributions. In the process, influential and powerful actors worked to make the engagement of smaller players, notably consumers and individual farmers, easier. As a new environmental management planning instrument, RPPLH not only reconstructed the playing field and redistributed roles and responsibilities to a wider set of actors, including various government agencies, but also re-established how those responsibilities should be taken; in other words, reframing how actors respond to environmental problems. The consistent summoning of stakes by the central actors of the DS organisation evolved into collective evaluation processes of governance goals. It also brought about diverse forms of responsibility and reflexivity over where respective actions can be meaningfully directed towards. The distributive agencies of instruments proved to lift some of the pressures placed on farmers, on the one hand, and consumers, on the other hand, to direct it towards actors placed in the middle of the value chain where decisions are seen as highly consequential. In this process, the assemblage also reached out to the larger assemblage where global relations between producing and consuming countries are to be taken into account. A desirable imaginary emerged around European "environmental soya" opening up a window of opportunity for Brazil, for instance, transitioning to organic soya and thus upscaling the current 10% achieved in this country.

Governance of emergence in AEG should aim to either distribute responsibilities proportionally to the actual capacity to influence the trajectory of the food and agriculture assemblages or rebalance power relations that lock these assemblages in unsustainable situations. In the first case, it implies reorienting governance away from its focus on individual responsibility and favourite targets, mostly individual consumers or farmers, to more risky and novel interventions across food and agriculture assemblages, targeting a diversity of actors, including the initiators of governance practices themselves. Indeed, governance practices are too often constructed in a way that limits the attribution of responsibility for outcomes to the governed, overlooking the role of the governors. This should be reversed. In the second case, the autonomisation of small players, such as farmers or consumers, becomes a tool for building more sustainable food futures. From an assemblage perspective, this autonomisation can only happen through alliances. Consequently, governance aims begin to favour the emergence of alliances and experimentations. In most cases, such an endeavour also means buffering the pressure exerted by power relations. In this sense, the *governance of emergence* automatically focuses on relational objectives, as relations are the fundamental architecture of assemblages.

Prioritising processual and relational objectives and outcomes

Measurable outputs, control of achievements, and sanctions in case of noncompliance play a central albeit overpowering role in most current environmental governance practices. While there are many reasons for defending the importance of improving the accountability of actors regarding environmentally harming practices and implementing "strong accountability" systems (Sareen & Wolf, 2021), an assemblage perspective calls for leaving more space for less controllable and unintended dimensions of change. The complexity of processes of change, their multiplicity and unpredictability call for a definition of governance objectives as a matter of creating paths towards a desirable future, rather than achieving predefined goals or adopting pre-identified practices. To transform an assemblage means to affect all relations— making new ones, breaking others, changing power balances—and opening up new possibilities. Concrete and measurable outcomes are, of course, important, and such an approach does not mean discarding any attempt to monitor changes. However, too often, a fundamental mistaken belief underpins many governance practices: that precise targets can be easily achieved if we design the right tools and that having precise goals *per se* is more efficient in achieving change.

Yet, at least in terms of sustainability, governance has failed in this endeavour (Arnouts & Arts, 2009; Miller & Rose, 1990). Indeed, prescribed practices do not provide the expected outcomes, and fixed and measurable objectives are rarely achieved, giving the impression of stagnation or failure of governance actions. This auto-generative diagnosis of failure can have a negative impact on motivations and the desire to pursue what becomes unachievable objectives.

More fundamentally, the focus on measurable outputs of governance objectifies and renders graspable some of the processes that emerge from a governance assemblage. However, simultaneously, it renders invisible many other processes that might develop in parallel. The logic of quantification and measuring becomes hegemonic to the extent that much of what is not measured and measurable does not count and is not taken into account. Assemblage thinking advocates for acknowledging and integrating existing and emerging alternative processes of change that overflow the boundary of precise objectives. Counting has its limits, however, and needs continuous recontextualisation. Otherwise, focusing on fixed and measurable, but always partial, objectives increases the risk highlighted by Park and Kramarz (2019) of a mismatch between governance means and governance ends, and therefore of losing sight of the fundamental objectives of environmental governance, to concentrate mainly on a follow-up of governance means—making instruments "work"—and forget a deeper follow-through of governance ends.

A *governance of emergence* moves the focus to relations and processes. It builds on the lesson that transformation happens through reconfigurations of relations and the generation of the new processes they include. If IP-Suisse has grown and become a significant contributor to the dissemination of the desire for and the enactment of more sustainable agricultural practices, it is because the organisation has developed strong relations of interdependence with many actors in value chains and the broader food and agriculture assemblage. The fundamental contribution of Donau Soja has been the development of a dense network of collaboration and the generation of thoughts around soya in Europe. In Indonesia, the apparent failure of RPPLH to fundamentally reform land planning and impact assessment in Indonesia should not hide the underlying changes in how diverse actors interact and collaborate.

This focus on relations is not limited to the human elements of the assemblage. As we have seen, the relation to bureaucratic instruments, soya as a plant, a seed, and a source of protein, or to data and maps deeply influences how assemblages form and evolve. To exemplify the importance of relations in transforming the fundamental processes guiding agri-environmental assemblages, we can draw on the work of scholars engaging with soil from the perspective of care (Puig de la Bellacasa, 2015; Krzywoszynska, 2019). As those authors highlight, soil exhaustion through agricultural practices goes hand in hand with a specific way of relating to soil as a mere support for human activity. Moving away from these processes of overexploitation of soil implies changing the quality of the relationship—from a logic of control to a logic of care and attentiveness. It also implies acknowledging and integrating into the web of relations around soil's diverse elements that have been ignored but are all essential to soil health, such as earthworms, insects, or fungi. While AEG instruments related to soil quality would target measurable biological and physical outcomes, without questioning how soil is integrated into webs of relations, a form of *governance of emergence* should target this kind of recon-figuration of relations that leads to a reorientation of fundamental processes. Indeed, the practice of using soybeans as cover crops has been forgotten, and the nitrogen-fixing property excluded as a count-able element.

Creating reflexive and processual methods for monitoring change

The first principle highlighted the importance of diversifying object-ives and outcomes to revert the prejudices against non-measurable outcomes and remain somewhat discerning because of their qualitative and relational nature. However, this call does not equal renouncing all kinds of accountability and monitoring of change. We have already highlighted the importance of reflexive governance. Reflexivity requires monitoring and feedback instruments and methods. However, these instruments and methods should not only be able to assess meas-urable outcomes but also be attuned to the identification of multiple and often unexpected processes, which escape usual monitoring but happen and matter nevertheless. For such an open and encompassing reflexive governance, the question becomes what kind of processes and relations are we initiating/supporting, and what kind of processes are we stopping or impeding? Again, this monitoring also requires the assessment of concrete and measurable effects; however, it does not stop there. Those quantitative measurements should be the first step and the means for more qualitative and dialogic monitoring.

This way of replacing reflexive governance within a complex landscape of actors and interventions echoes what Voß and Kemp (2006: 7) call second-order governance, understood as "a procedural approach towards reflecting the interdependencies, understanding aggregate effects of specialised concepts and strategies, and engaging in the modulation of ongoing societal developments by establishing links and organising problem-oriented communication and interaction among distributed steering activities". However, the everyday framing on governance highlights the fact that this reflexive engagement with the effects of governance cannot be restricted to the perspective of the people initiating governance actions and the experts consulted. Therefore, a *governance of emergence* requires a reflexive and processual monitoring which seeks and welcomes the multiple and diverse experiences of the actors involved in the governance assemblage. This includes, but is not limited to, the active and direct participation of the "stakeholders"—following the now classical category used in the governance lingo. The assemblage approach clearly indicates that the actors concerned and affected by governance practices are far more numerous. If the ambition of integrating all the possible perspectives would be unrealistic, a fundamental openness to the diversity of perspectives is necessary and of crucial importance, as confirmed by the critical discussion around the UN Food System Summit and the implications of who was or was not invited (Canfield et al., 2021).

Acknowledging and integrating diverse perspectives consequently highlights the probable dissensus on objectives and effects and, therefore, the inevitably political dimension not only of governance practices but also of the monitoring process. The inevitable political dimension—in a broad sense of the encounter and confrontation of a wider range of worldviews resulting in productive dissensus—has been well commented on by Castree and colleagues (2021) in the context of global environmental assessments, as a central piece of "wicked assessments" answering "wicked problems". For the authors, environmental assessment opens to a "space of existential choice", which is a "space that's overflowing with debatable framings of society, with politics not merely policy options, and with strategic choices not only operational ones" (Castree et al., 2021: 69). This space mirrors the space of possibility in assemblage thinking. In this sense, reflexive and processual monitoring for AEG is not so much a place of external and neutral knowledge production but also, above all, a political space where diverse perspectives meet. Castree and colleagues describe these politics of assessment as "diverse, ordered conceptions of the world that marry diagnosis with critique, analysis with evaluation, evidence with argument" (ibid.: 72). A *governance of emergence* expands this integration of the subjective and political by highlighting the dimension of affects through the notion of desire, not just as a human complication of assessment, but rather as a central feature of the dynamics of assemblage. Desire emphasises that the diversity of perspectives and agendas is not an obstacle to a—otherwise elusive—consensus as a precondition for generating change, but rather drives the coming together of actors following diverse interests. What emerges from governance originates fundamentally in this convergence.

When talking with actors of the IP-Suisse assemblage, one can observe that sparks of transformation emerge not so much, thanks to the capacity of the biodiversity point system to reflect effective environmental benefits, nor in the sense of control allowed by the certification scheme. Rather, they appear in a general vision where farmers can still see themselves as good producers while doing something for the environment, in the collective experimentation made possible by the gathering of diverse actors, and in the actors' enthusiasm for exploring new possibilities. In other words, sustainability needs collective desire. Donau Soja meetings, as governance practices, mobilise desires into affective territories where imaginaries and desires are co-constituted. They require sophisticated setups that allow people to move to places and get together, to exchange insights, to sense and experience, imagine and make sense together, and finally to take action. This process of collective reflexive engagement is more than a dialogical exercise where ideas are communicated from one to another. It is not knowledge transfer, nor is it capacity building in a classical sense. It has consequences. Here, inclusive governance pays off. Experts from different fields have a rare chance to mingle and get better at grasping the complexity of issues. A collective goal-sharing exercise takes place. More than expected results emerge. This coming together of actors is also visible in the case of RPPLH, where the more stringent planning instrument is not the one that drives the planning process. It is instead the fact that through this new space of possibility, actors (different government sectors, academics, and professionals) can find a way to channel their wishes and inspirations and, indeed, their desires on how environmental governance ought to manifest. And yet, it is not only the human actors that pursue their desires. Nature, through layers of data and proxies, brings its desire to the table, allowing actors to change their viewpoint on the environment.

Desire also questions the role and limitations of expert knowledge in guiding governance and change. In the *governance of emergence*, expertise is obviously more than technical and fact-based. It not only helps nurture the reflexive process through scientific monitoring but also contributes to the emergence of new desires and existential spaces. Scientific experts, among other actors, have indeed important arguments to bring in the formation of collective desires. If we follow Gergen's (2015: 294) call for a paradigm shift in research—from producing a reflection of the world to "illuminate what is" to contributing to the formation of the future and "create what is to become"—we could even say that this role is primary. However, scientists have collectively developed little competences in reflexively co-constructing desire with the other actors. Therefore, the *governance of emergence* is also about a change in the culture of expertise.

Targeting attractors to influence spaces of possibility

Moving away from precise objectives in terms of the adoption of specific practices or the achievement of measurable outcomes requires redefining the target of governance action in order to propose answers that match the importance of the sustainability challenges facing food and agriculture. From an assemblage perspective, innovations and changes can sometimes be a means to actually maintain as much as possible the current state of things and to keep the same trajectory. Because changes happen constantly and introduce new unsettling elements in the assemblage, often the reaction is to voluntarily take action to avoid destabilisation, restore what has been lost, and keep moving in the same direction. This is all fine and legitimate, when stability is the objective. However, when governance aims at a change of direction, a switch in priorities, or a re-foundation of relations—as should be the case with AEG—then change should be transformative. The definition of transformation we offered in Chapter 5—as *a deep redefinition of the space of possibility resulting from a reorientation of attractors and the emergence of new capacities*—provides the first insights into how to achieve this: by targeting attractors and capacities. This means that while concrete, technical, and practical elements are most of the time part of the process of change, the production of new imaginaries and desires is also essential.

Attractors, imaginaries, and desires are not the same thing, but they are deeply entangled. They work together in redirecting the trajectory of an assemblage by shaping the basin of attraction. Thinking of governance with the notion of attractor in mind draws our attention to how dominant narratives and imaginaries rooted in material arrangements help consolidate a status quo despite perpetual changes and innovations. This is where a *governance of emergence* is open to alternative futures and gets inspiration from experimentations and "real utopias" (Wright, 2020). Prefigurative imaginaries constitute the fertile ground in which new attractors can take root. However, attractors are not only made of desires and ideals but also of material arrangements. In this sense, generating new desires is not enough if this does not include a reopening of concrete possibilities. This double dimension of governance, with desires and meanings, on the one hand, and materiality in governance, on the other hand, is pointed to by Buchanan (2021: 127) when he says that conceiving policy as an assemblage implies "seeing it in terms of the kinds of arrangements and orderings it makes possible and even more importantly the complex and not always fully disclosed set of expectations it entails". This is why a *governance of emergence* means fundamentally engaging reflexivity with this double nature to impact attractors.

When diverse actors of the soya value chain meet at the initiative of DS, they do not resolve the tensions and disagreements that might exist between them. Nevertheless, from these meetings emerge new visions of possible soya futures, which reorient these diverse perspectives towards a shared horizon without implying a unification of all objectives and desires. At the same time, investments in infrastructures for the development of a renewed soya value chain in Europe have made new collaborations and relations possible. While we mentioned that actors did find a consensus on how to better manage the environment through RPPLH, it does not mean that all actors have the same objective. Each actor still pursues their desires and interests, while at the same time confronting the others over contradicting goals. No patch of land can be used for two purposes at once, so only those actors (agricultural, settlement, public work, or environmental agencies) that can make their case heard would be allowed to push through their plan on that patch of land. However, what this means is that the coming together of different desires is what makes the assemblage vibrant in ways that shape the

new environmental management plan. Likewise, when retailers, industrial bakeries, mills, IP-Suisse, and farmers collaborate to develop a
pesticide-free grain value chain, they do not aim for the same objectives, nor build on the same appreciation of the situation. Neither do
they share the visions of the activist who launched a political movement
for banning pesticides from Swiss agriculture. However, all of them
brought in the assemblage desires that resulted in a significant change
and worked to make it possible, by adapting standards, separating flows,
or experimenting with new agricultural practices.

These last references to our case studies also show clearly that
AEG engages in transformative work when diverse instruments and
actions converge, often unintentionally, towards a shared direction.
In this sense, doing *governance of emergence* means embracing its
relational nature. Actors of governance should therefore have an acute
sense of how their practice participates in a wider governance assemblage, in order to look for alliances and synergies, and counter lock-
in situations. This assemblage-attuned engagement in governance
goes beyond coordination to mitigate uncertainty and antagonism. In
actuality, it is more like developing the skills and attention needed to
navigate uncharted futures.

Conclusion: a governance of emergence as a new attractor for AEG

In this concluding chapter, we have engaged with what we consider as
the contributions of assemblage thinking in regenerating the practice
of governance. We have built the argument that assemblage thinking
can participate in the transformation needed in our agri-food systems.
Laying the emphasis on the notion of emergence and capacities,
assemblage thinking contributes to a paradigmatic change and an epistemological turn in how we address unpredictability in the practice
of governance. Without providing ready-to-use instruments and good
practices, we hope to have offered deep anchors for the foundations of
a *governance of emergence*. We share this call with all those who take
a stance—through reflexive governance, distributed responsibility,
global environmental assessments, and similar engagements—in
favour of rejuvenating the answers, actions, and attitudes our societies
embody in relation to the burning challenges faced by our food and
agriculture futures. We contend that assemblage thinking provides a
framing that relates and articulates these elements.

What emerges from this theoretical assemblage, we argue, is more than the sum of its elements. Redistributed responsibilities, processual and relational objectives, reflexive and processual monitoring, and attractors as targets work together in a *governance of emergence*. We offer it as a new paradigm for transformative AEG. We regard the translation of these four principles into actual governance practices as already rooted in currently unfolding efforts and manifold experimentations which diminish the grip of other attractors pulling in different and sometimes opposing directions. Our objective is, therefore, emancipatory, in that we offer this *governance of emergence* as a new attractor for redirecting AEG, nurturing a desire for renewed practices and logics in the wide and global AEG assemblage. In this process, our own desire is to now encounter others' desires. As multiple others have made it possible for reflexive engagement to be developed in this book, so multiple others are needed for the emergence and enactment of this *governance of emergence*.

References

Arnold, N., Brunori, G., Dessein, J., Galli, F., Ghosh, R., Loconto, A. M., & Maye, D. (2022). Governing food futures: towards a 'responsibility turn' in food and agriculture. *Journal of Rural Studies* 89: 82–86.

Arnouts, R., & Arts, B. (2009). Environmental governance failure: The "dark side" of an essentially optimistic concept. In B. Arts, A. Lagendijk, & H. van Houtum (Eds.), *The Desoriented State. Shifts in Governmentality, Territoriality and Governance* (pp. 201–228). Berlin: Springer.

Barnett, C., Cloke, P., Clarke, N., & Malpass, A. (2011). *Globalizing Responsibility: The Political Rationalities of Ethical Consumption.* Chichester: Wiley.

Bennett, J. (2010). *Vibrant Matter: A Political Ecology of Things.* Durham and London: Duke University Press.

Buchanan, I. (2021). *Assemblage Theory and Method.* London/ New York: Bloomsbury.

Canfield, M. C., Duncan, J., & Claeys, P. (2021). Reconfiguring food systems governance: the UNFSS and the battle over authority and legitimacy. *Development* 64(3): 181–191.

Castree, N., Bellamy, R., & Osaka, S. (2021). The future of global environmental assessments: making a case for fundamental change. *The Anthropocene Review* 8(1): 56–82.

Evans, D., Welch, D., & Swaffield, J. (2017). Constructing and mobilizing 'the consumer': responsibility, consumption and the politics of sustainability. *Environment and Planning A: Economy and Space* 49(6): 1396–1412.

Gergen, K. J. (2015). From mirroring to world-making: research as future forming. *Journal for the Theory of Social Behaviour* 45(3): 287–310.

Krzywoszynska, A. (2019). Caring for soil life in the Anthropocene: the role of attentiveness in more-than-human ethics. *Transactions of the Institute of British Geographers* 44(4): 661–675.

Lea, T. (2014). "From little things, big things grow": the unfurling of wild policy. *E-Flux* 58: 1–8.

Maye, D., Kirwan, J., & Brunori, G. (2019). Ethics and responsibilisation in agri-food governance: the single-use plastics debate and strategies to introduce reusable coffee cups in UK retail chains. *Agriculture and Human Values* 36(2): 301–312.

Miller, P., & Rose, N. (1990). Governing economic life. *Economy and Society* 19(1): 1–31.

Park, S., & Kramarz, T. (Eds.). (2019). *Global Environmental Governance and the Accountability Trap*. Cambridge, MA: MIT Press.

Portes, A. (2000). The hidden abode: sociology as analysis of the unexpected: 1999 presidential address. *American Sociological Review* 65(1): 1–18.

Puig de la Bellacasa, M. (2015). Making time for soil: technoscientific futurity and the pace of care. *Social Studies of Science* 45(5): 691–716.

Rip, A. (2006). A co-evolutionary approach to reflexive governance – and its ironies. In V. Jan-Peter, D. Bauknecht, & R. Kemp (Eds.). *Reflexive Governance for Sustainable Development* (pp. 82–100). Cheltenham, UK/ Northampton, MA: Edward Elgar.

Sareen, S., & Wolf, S. A. (2021). Accountability and sustainability transitions. *Ecological Economics* 185: 107056.

Scott, J. C. (1998). *Seeing Like a State: How Certain Schemes to Improve the Human Condition Have Failed*. New Haven, CT: Yale University Press.

Shove, E. (2010). Beyond the ABC: climate change policy and theories of social change. *Environment and Planning A: Economy and Space* 42(6): 1273–1285.

Stirling, A. (2015). Emancipating transformations: from controlling 'the transition' to culturing plural radical progress. In I. Scoones, M. Leach, & P. Newell (Eds.). *The Politics of Green Transformations* (pp. 54–67). New York and London: Routledge.

Voß, J.-P., & Kemp, R. (2006). Sustainability and reflexive governance: introduction. In J.-P. Voß, D. Bauknecht, & R. Kemp (Eds.). *Reflexive Governance for Sustainable Development* (pp. 3–28). Cheltenham, UK/ Northampton, MA: Edward Elgar.

Walker, G., & Shove, E. (2007). Ambivalence, sustainability and the governance of socio-technical transitions. *Journal of Environmental Policy & Planning* 9(3–4): 213–225.

Wright, E. O. (2020). *Envisioning Real Utopias*. London: Verso Books.

Index

For Product Safety Concerns and Information please contact our EU
representative GPSR@taylorandfrancis.com
Taylor & Francis Verlag GmbH, Kaufingerstraße 24, 80331 München, Germany